Jay
Love is the
answer! Gabe 2/10-19

GIVING LOVE A VOICE

Book One: Lessons in Health

Gabriel Richards

BALBOA
PRESS

A DIVISION OF HAY HOUSE

Balboa Press books may be ordered through booksellers or by contacting:

Balboa Press
A Division of Hay House
1663 Liberty Drive
Bloomington, IN 47403
www.balboapress.com
1 (877) 407-4847

Because of the dynamic nature of the Internet, any web addresses or links contained in this book may have changed since publication and may no longer be valid. The views expressed in this work are solely those of the author and do not necessarily reflect the views of the publisher, and the publisher hereby disclaims any responsibility for them.

The author of this book does not dispense medical advice or prescribe the use of any technique as a form of treatment for physical, emotional, or medical problems without the advice of a physician, either directly or indirectly. The intent of the author is only to offer information of a general nature to help you in your quest for emotional and spiritual well-being. In the event you use any of the information in this book for yourself, which is your constitutional right, the author and the publisher assume no responsibility for your actions.

Any people depicted in stock imagery provided by Getty Images are models, and such images are being used for illustrative purposes only. Certain stock imagery © Getty Images.

Print information available on the last page.

ISBN: 978-1-9822-1143-1 (sc)
ISBN: 978-1-9822-1144-8 (hc)
ISBN: 978-1-9822-1145-5 (e)

Library of Congress Control Number: 2018910404

Balboa Press rev. date: 09/20/2018

PREFACE

What you are about to read is a true story written from my perspective. Just a few names have been changed or eliminated to protect the innocent or guilty, whichever they may be.

I choose to write this book at the suggestion of many people. After relating the story of my wife's illness and the lessons learned to church groups, civic groups and others, all too often there would be a request from those present that I put the story in book form. People found the story fascinating and the lessons learned of value. The events were painful, the lessons profound.

These events include the onset of what was to ultimately paralyze her and the three consecutive hospital stays of about three months each. I have included a couple of years after returning from the Philippines and the ashram where we visited the spiritual healers in the mountains outside Bagio City. Not only was that a key part of the healing process, but it also sets the scene for another book in the *Chapters of Life* series.

This book also covers the decade from 1972 to 1982 as I feel it necessary to help a reader understand the depth of love between us and why I would simply never give up. We have also achieved some unbelievable financial accomplishments as well as several rather significant setbacks, and those will be the subjects of book 2. This is a story of how love and faith can overcome nearly any challenge.

It is written as it happened with as much accuracy as I can remember. I have asked not only my children but also extended family and friends to fill in parts that I may have blanked out of my memory. My children say there are periods that are just gone from their memory cards too. The human mind is amazing in the way it will protect us from things that hurt so badly we simply could not relive them.

As I look back, I am not sorry about anything that happened. Of course, I would rather not have had some of those experiences, but my life would not be the same had I not endured each one. It seems that my lot in life has been to learn things the hard way. It is my sincere wish that many will learn from our experiences and live lives filled with love, health, wealth, and peace of mind without all the hard lessons.

For those of you who are in the middle of your hard lessons, I contend that there is always a way out. The pendulum of life will swing both ways, and the farther it swings one way, the farther it swings the other. Our story is proof that with love, faith, and the right attitude, people can overcome almost any challenge. To love and to be loved are among the greatest gifts in life. I think the best gift we can give the people in our lives is to be healthy and happy. We are here to learn to love without conditions. For true healing you must first learn to love yourself no matter what your circumstances. I hope to not only identify the lifestyles, attitudes, and/or the general lack of understanding that may contribute to the onset of illness but also offer solutions that have worked for us. At the end I offer *a few basics* that I feel have real value. However, adopting the basics to overcome illness is one thing. It is much better to avoid illness altogether. We have proven that adopting a lifestyle that ensures health is preferable to finding solutions to an illness that could have been avoided in the first place.

This book is primarily about lessons in health—why it was necessary to study the subject and keep health a priority in your life. The story covers about a fifteen-year period. Interestingly, it has been more than forty-five years since that shot of us on the cover was taken.

CONTENTS

CHAPTER 1

The Outset

Toward the end of the day, as I often did, I made my last stop at our door company, Regional Door and Hardware. When I entered the office, my secretary, Debbie, told me that my wife had come in just a bit earlier and that something was very wrong. Debbie had no idea what was going on with Jill, but my brother Daniel, who worked there, had taken her to a doctor's office. Debbie gave me the address.

That entire day I'd had a feeling in my gut that I was missing something. I immediately knew it had been Jill trying to connect with me. Since our very first conversation, we had always had a deep connection. How could I have let business consume my mind so much that I missed the tug on my heart? All of a sudden, I understood the business meetings and deals made earlier today would mean nothing if my wife was not okay. I figured out the shortest route to the doctor's office and wasted little time getting there. As I drove, I thought, *What the hell could have happened? Jill should have been at Tahoe all day. Why was she in Reno?*

As I reached the doctor's office, my wife and my brother were coming down the steps, and Dan was helping Jill keep her balance. As soon as I was close enough, she latched onto me intensely, buried her head in my neck, and began sobbing like a frightened child. It was as if she had been holding it back and could now let go.

Dan handed me a piece of paper. "These are the directions given to me by the doctor inside. This will get you to a neurologist's office. He will be waiting there for you. If you need me, you know where to look." I knew the Ponderosa was his favorite watering hole, and I could tell he needed a beer, maybe a couple.

I had to help Jill into the car. At this point, she was disoriented and unstable, confused as to where she was and where she had been. All she could remember was driving around most of the day, trying to find something familiar. She remembered not being able to keep her car in the correct lane. She felt her mind was slowly leaving her body. To be sure, something was very wrong, and we had no idea what it could be. Jill was frightened. I could really feel that on a deep level. Why was she so unstable?

I looked at the note and saw an address close to the hospital I knew all too well.

Usually in this type of situation, I somehow had the ability to shut off emotion. By removing myself from my feelings, I could get clarity and gain perspective so I could take the right action. This one was pushing my limit. It didn't take long to find the doctor's office.

The young lady at the front desk led us to a room right away, and I was glad to see the doctor arrive in moments. He began with a series of questions and then conducted some simple tests. The doctor asked Jill questions she should have known, including "Who is the president?" "President of what?" she asked. I remember that like it was yesterday. Most of the questions sounded to me like a sobriety test. *Do you know where you are? Do you know what day it is? What is your birth date?* Jill just looked at him. She could not come up with answers to his questions. He tested the strength in her arms, first the right and then the left. He asked her to touch her nose, and she couldn't. The doctor may have been a highly trained specialist, but he had an abrasive manner that did not help the situation. After all that, he said, "I think we're dealing with a stroke, but I need a CAT scan. I'll meet you at the hospital."

I decided it would be easier to carry Jill to the car rather than help her walk. It was a short distance to the emergency entrance. They met us with a wheelchair. She was taken to a room for the brain scan, but I couldn't enter. There was nothing to do now but wait.

When the neurologist finally came to the waiting room, I could not discern if he was concerned or more perplexed.

"Mr. Richards, your wife has suffered a stroke. The CAT scan clearly shows an aneurism. A blood vessel on the right hemisphere has burst, and there is considerable bleeding and some brain damage. How much we do not know. I want to admit her for observation and some tests. We need to know why a healthy thirty-two-year-old has suffered an aneurism. We will do further testing in the morning."

"You don't suppose, Doc, this has anything to do with the removal of a bunion on her foot a few days ago, do you? It was simple. In the office and out again. Didn't take long."

He raised his eyebrow. "It could. We'll find out."

As Jill was transferred to the neuroglial floor, I took care of the admission paperwork. By the time I got to the sixth floor, Jill was sleeping. It had been a very hard day for her. I took the time to call home. I talked to our eldest daughter, LaVon, and I told her Mom was having some tests run in the hospital and that I would be home late.

I sat on the hospital bed, held her hand, and spent some serious time in prayer. My prayer was that the doctors would find what had caused this and fix it and that she would heal soon.

Sometime after midnight I determined there was nothing I could do for Jill. I had three daughters at home, and I had to be there for them. I went to my car, sat behind the wheel for a while, and thought, *Kids at home. Wife in the hospital. Where should I be?*

Usually, I enjoyed the drive from Reno over the Mt. Rose Pass home to Incline Village on the north shore of Lake Tahoe. Thinking about driving away from the hospital under these circumstances was painful. As I drove, the words just kept ringing in my head, "Brain damage. How much we don't know."

On the way to the summit at the eight-thousand-foot elevation marker, there was an area where I could pull off the highway and look over the valley and Reno far below. Tears were making it hard to see, so I pulled over, got out, and sat on a guardrail post. I tried prayer but only found I was mad at God. My understanding was that if he did not cause this, he at least allowed it. *How could he let this happen?*

It had been ten wonderful years to the month since I had met my beautiful wife and not long after made a lifetime commitment to her and her two daughters. I thought about the first time I met her and all that had happened since.

CHAPTER 2

REAL COMMUNICATION

I met Jill shortly after I moved to Reno. I was driving home from work, thinking about the recent move and how fortunate I was to have this job, but then again, I wondered if I would ever come to terms with living in a city. It was 1972, and at 4,500 feet in elevation, Reno was home to almost fifty thousand people, including my family. This was a big city compared to where I had come from. I moved with Dottie, my wife of twelve years at the time, a son named Abe who was almost eleven, and our seven-year-old daughter LaVon. I had high hopes this would be a whole new start for a troubled relationship. Even though city life had little appeal for me, it offered many opportunities not found in any small town for a seasoned journeyman carpenter like me. For eight of the past twelve years, racing motorcycles had become the perfect diversion to an empty marriage. The people who raced offered a subculture that I enjoyed. They were an odd but tight group, and the four other guys I teamed up with were focused on being the best in the sport. Reno had also offered me the opportunity to turn professional at racing, and that would offset the negatives of living in a city.

The Robinhood Apartment complex, our temporary home, was on the south end of Reno, and we could access our unit by a long drive that skirted a horse ranch. I drove down South Virginia Street and turned west on Robinhood Drive. What came into view as I eased up the drive that warm July afternoon was absolutely breathtaking. Just in front of me a lush green pasture bordered by a white fence with flowers at its base, and I saw the Sierra Nevada Mountains partly covered with winter snow in the background. Just to my left, there was a well-groomed and extremely handsome horse. I was reminded of my older brother Rafael's mare, Ginger, a beautiful animal almost sixteen hands, well defined with a high spirit. I was too young to cut her loose, but when Rafael did, she could run like the wind. As I approached this horse now, I could tell that this guy was bigger and had magnificent definition. To complete the scene, the most beautiful young lady dressed in an all-white high-neck sleeveless top and matching pants was feeding him carrots. As she reached to stroke the animal, her brown hair fell halfway down her back. I slowed the van to take it all in, wishing I had my camera with the wide-angle lens. If I could have captured this on film, I could have sold a lot of copies. Everything in view was unbelievably beautiful.

As I slowed the van, she turned to look. I did a bit of a double take. *Was Elvis and his wife in south Reno on a ranch?* As I got a bit closer, I saw that it wasn't Pricilla, but she looked pretty close.

I pulled to the left side of the road and stopped directly across from the apartment complex. I leaned out the window and asked, "Is he your horse?"

"No," she replied. "I love all animals, and I was just letting this one know."

In one graceful move, she retrieved a carrot from a bag at her feet, pulled his head close to her, and fed it to him.

"I understand your love for animals. Some of my best friends in this life have four legs. I just moved from Mammoth Mountain, and I felt it would be better for the animal to leave my Saint Bernard behind. Loved that dog, but I knew she would not be happy living at less than eight thousand feet, so I just gave her away, little whisky keg and all. One of the hardest things I ever did. Not sure I can live down here and deal with life in a city myself."

Never taking her hand from the horse, she looked me right in the eye, and after a pause said, "The move must have been really important." She said it with so much compassion.

Even though I tried not to show the feelings welling up inside me, she apparently understood how deeply I cared about the things I loved so much and had left behind. It wasn't so much what she said or how she said it. There was something else, something unspoken.

I replied, "It was important to me. We'll just have to see how it goes."

"I recently moved to Reno myself. I think it's beautiful here with the mountains so close and the river running through the middle. To me it has a small-town feel. You'll get used to it. I'm sure of it," She said it with such conviction. I had to wonder where it came from.

"Ma'am, I would like to think you're right, but Bishop, California, is the biggest town I ever lived in, with less than three thousand souls, and that was more than ten times bigger than where I came from.

She picked up another carrot for the horse, fed him, and turned to look at the mountains. "My parents moved to the Village of June Lake just this side of Mammoth Mountain after I left home. The entire region is so majestic, more than beautiful. I understand why you would love it."

Turning back, her green eyes focused on me. "So what's with the van? It's too nice to be a delivery truck."

"Well, I have an unhealthy relationship with my iron horses, so they're always with me in the back. I race motorcycles, and for me, it's pure enjoyment."

She kind of cocked her head and looked at me as if to say, "Are you okay?" I could tell she didn't understand my love for motorcycles. She said so much with her eyes.

Turning her attention back to the horse, she said, "So you race motorcycles … Do you have a name?"

"It's Gabriel, just like the angel. I say it that way so people remember it. But you can call me Gabe. How about you?"

She responded, "I go by Jill. It's a middle name. My mom chose Deborah, and my dad wanted Jill, so that is what I got. I never felt like Deborah, so I became Jill. It works for me. I'd like to talk more, but I have to get back to my children. I have a friend watching my girls while I take a break. It has been nice."

Lifting the brim of my hat, I said, "Pleasure has been all mine." I bid her a good day, swung the van around, and entered the complex. I found my assigned spot, shut the engine down, and reclined the seat. I sat there for a minute, trying to process what had just taken place. I thought to myself, *Okay, I understand an appreciation for a girl in her early twenties with green eyes, long brown hair, and a great shape. But I had kind of a weird feeling like I had met her somewhere. No, a lady with that beauty I would not forget.* I thought about how she seemed to know better than me what I was feeling. That almost made me uncomfortable.

I had never encountered someone who could seemingly read my thoughts or understand what I was feeling, and why did that make me feel uncomfortable? I guessed it was the unspoken communication that made me uneasy. I couldn't remember ever experiencing that.

I couldn't think about that right now. Just as soon as I checked in with my wife, I needed to pull the speedway bike out and get it cleaned up and ready for tomorrow night's race.

As I entered the apartment, my wife said, "I got a swing shift job, and I found a young lady to watch Abe and LaVon. I start work tomorrow."

Surprised, I said, "What is the job, and where did you find someone to watch the kids?"

"I'm going back to work as an operator. Same job, different phone company. I met this girl at the pool. She has two kids of her own and lives in the first lower apartment on the other side of the pool. She and her husband are waiting for a home to be completed, so they'll be here for a few months. She is a full-time mom, and she won't mind watching Abe and LaVon until you get home. She'll have the kids tomorrow when you get home from work, so this evening I'll introduce you."

"If you are working swing, you'll miss most of the speedway races. The kids will have to be in the stands by themselves."

"Not really," she said. "I checked with Nancy Lee, and she will be happy to keep an eye on them. Larry will be racing, so Abe and LaVon can hang out with the Lee kids."

"You're right, the kids will be fine. I like it when Abe spends time with Troy and Kelly. Those kids seem to be a bit more rational than Abe. It all works for me if it works for you. I'm going to get the speedway bike ready."

After dinner we went down the stairs to the first apartment on the other side of the pool. When the door opened, there was Jill— dark hair, green eyes, olive skin, and simply stunning.

I said, "Hello again, lady with the middle name Jill. Looks like you will have four kids tomorrow. Think you can deal with a ten-year-old boy who has a habit of giving his seven-year-old sister a hard way to go?"

She smiled with kind of a twinkle in her eye. "I think so."

I turned to Dottie and explained that Jill and I had met. I thought she might be concerned, but she wasn't.

Jill was twenty-two, and her daughters Lori and Lisa were two and three and a half years old. Her husband had a delivery route for a major bread company. He seemed a bit detached, but we still had a very pleasant conversation with Jill. It began with some small talk and turned quickly to our philosophy on life and raising children. After an interesting exchange, we all agreed that she would watch Abe and LaVon at the pool the next day after work. We also agreed that we would all get together for dinner soon.

As we walked home, we talked about what it was that made the young woman so special. We agreed she was beautiful, but that was overshadowed by her sweet spirit, her wisdom, and her warmth.

"I knew you would approve," she said. We both felt the children would be in good hands.

What I didn't tell her about was Jill's uncanny ability to connect with my thoughts.

The next day when I arrived at the pool after work, all the kids were having a wonderful time. Jill sat on the edge of the pool in a two-piece swimsuit, watching the children play. The vision was like something out of a magazine, but I had always thought that to look like that, the photo had to be touched up. Her hair, eyes, and skin suggested maybe she was Italian or Spanish. It was hard for me not to stare, but in moments she started with the questions. She kept me so busy answering questions that I hardly had time to catch my breath. I think for the first time ever I almost ignored my kids for a time.

I told her we purchased our first home when my wife was eighteen and I was twenty-two. I did it by working three jobs, construction from seven in the morning to three thirty. I just had enough time to grab a bite and get to the Richfield gas station by four o'clock, where I pumped gas, changed tires, and did minor auto repair until nine in the evening. There was just enough time to drive to the radio station during the nine o'clock news, and at nine-fifteen until midnight, I worked as a DJ with my own rock-and-roll show. I was able to keep weekends open for my motorcycles.

"Sounds to me like the family life may have suffered," she said. "Owning a home shouldn't be a drag on the relationship,"

"At the time I thought owning a home would help a relationship that was suffering. But you're right. It didn't."

I shared that one of my goals was to at least supplement my income by racing motorcycles. That was also a completely foreign world to her. She had never really known anyone who rode motorcycles, let alone raced them for money. I told her that as a carpenter, I was paid by the piece, and as with my professional racing, I was paid only by results—nothing else. I never liked working by the hour and felt being self-employed would be by far the best way to support myself. I told her about the first business I was part owner of—a motorcycle shop in Bishop. The owner of the shop was my sponsor and paid my racing costs. Having a winning motorcycle was good for business, and I won a lot. He convinced me to buy in as part owner, which seemed like a good idea. I soon found out that his wife totally ran his life and that it was her plan to run mine. I sold my interest in the bike shop and went back to building. Not long after that, I was presented with an opportunity to buy half interest in a property that had a restaurant, gift shop, service station, and two homes. The restaurant had a beer and wine license. It wasn't long after taking over the business that my partner in this business (a guy I knew for a number of years) started drinking the profits. I did not drink, but he did ... a lot. Again, I sold my interest and went back to construction in the town of Mammoth Lakes.

In Reno, I would not have to deal nearly as much with building in the snow. Plus the work was all fast-paced and high-production building, and I liked that kind of construction best. I tried to be vague, adding that I hoped the move would be good for the home life as well.

As she had rarely attended church and had no religious convictions, she was most interested in mine, which I shared with her. My parents turned a garage on their property into a church they called the Pioneer Chapel. They were both ordained ministers, and my older brother was the full-time pastor of the chapel. This was a Pentecostal church. It was always a struggle for me to reconcile in my mind the way they taught the Bible. What I read in the Bible worked for me, but their interpretation seemed a bit odd. I later joined the Baptist church in Bishop, and my role became that of a mentor to the younger teenage boys. We had a group called the Boys Brigade, and I tried to keep them busy in their spare time and serve as a role model for them.

It was never my plan to be a carpenter. Carpentry was going to be what I did to get my commercial pilot's license and become a commercial pilot. Getting married curtailed that plan.

Two hours went by in a flash, and then it was time for her to return to her apartment and prepare dinner for her family. I watched her as she walked away with the grace of an athlete and the confidence of a woman who knew exactly who she was and yet still somehow retained the charm of a little girl.

As I sat there for a while, I realized she now knew a great deal about me, my family, my siblings, my religion, my job as a carpenter and how I went about that, everything. I knew very little about her. I did know she was raised in the Los Angeles area, where there were millions of people, and I was raised in the country, where the only town close by had a population of fewer than two hundred. She didn't know towns that small existed until her parents moved to the Village of June Lake.

West Point, California, was the only town even close to where we lived. The town survived on the economy created by the local lumber mill.

In the mid-1950s, if there was a hardship in the family, it was possible for a lad to obtain a regular driver's license at age fourteen. Otherwise, sixteen was the legal age. There was no welfare back then, and my mother was raising four boys by herself. By this time, my sister Connie was married and had started a family of her own. To some degree, we lived off the land with help from friends, neighbors, and Rudy Brickman, who owned the general store in West Point. Rudy supplied basics for our family and put it on a tab. I think it was his way of paying it forward. So we qualified as hardship.

When I was four and five years of age, my father would place me on the fuel tank of his Harley between his knees, and we would ride the mountain roads together. That was before he got on that Harley one day by himself, rode north, and was never heard from again. I knew one thing for sure. We were from two completely different worlds. Tomorrow I would ask the questions.

My normal job as a piecework carpenter had no set hours. As long as I produced a reasonable amount of completed product each week, I could pretty much come and go as I pleased. There was no time clock to punch. So I left work a bit early the next day because I had many questions to ask her. She was fascinating to talk with. It may have been that she heard every word I said or totally understood every thought I was trying to convey or asked me to restate it in a way that she could. This was something I had never experienced. She looked up as the gate closed behind me.

"You're off early today. Is everything okay?"

I didn't want her to even think I was there early because I was anxious to continue our conversation, and I figured the best way to skirt a question was to ask a question.

I looked at the book she had just put down and asked, "Do you read a lot?"

"Reading has always been a passion ever since I was small. I usually finish about a book a week. Now that I have children, I don't have as much time to read as I did when I was younger, but my kids are worth it."

"So what is it you are you reading?

"Oh, this book is on Western religion, something I don't know much about. You talked a lot yesterday about your religious convictions, and that made me curious. I've had this book for some time, and I've been meaning to get to it."

That answer puzzled me. I remembered that in our conversation yesterday, she'd mentioned her close relationship with God.

While I was formulating a question, LaVon pulled me away in an effort to play some underwater tag. She wasn't used to sharing me with anyone, not even her mother. I could tell she was not of a mind to let me do anything but pay attention to her. After a few rounds of tag, I shot from the bottom out of the water, landed by Jill, and asked, "So with no religious teaching, how do you know about God?"

"It never occurred to me to ask someone else about God because ever since I can remember, I've always had a close relationship with what I considered to be a heavenly being. My communication has always been very direct and very real. To me, God is everywhere, keeps the planets in place, and makes each flower grow, and by the way, has no gender."

I told LaVon I needed a break as I had to ask Jill some questions. She turned, did a cartwheel, and disappeared under the water.

From there the conversation went deep.

She had an interesting take on the laws of nature and how that tied in with her view of spirituality. She said she got her view on it all and why things are the way they are from her grandmother. I wanted to know about her grandmother. She said that her grandmother was Spanish and that her maiden name was Francis Perez. She had worked most all her life as a housekeeper, cook, and caregiver. She had never heard her grandmother raise her voice. She was always happy and at peace.

Jill was aware that somehow every one of her grandmother's eight children and all fourteen grandchildren thought he or she was Grandma's favorite. It did not take possessions to make her happy. For her it was the relationships with both family and friends and quality time with each. Jill's grandmother always put others first. And while not religious, she maintained a close personal relationship with God that seemed to be her foundation for life. I had to wonder about this woman Jill spoke so kindly of—who she was and where she had learned what she knew. I had a yearning to know how she could be happy with so very little in this day and age. I told Jill I would love to meet her grandmother one day.

Jill started working at the age of twelve, babysitting and ironing, and at fourteen, she went to work at W. T. Grant's. As part of her job, she was in charge of taking care of the birds and fish that were for sale. With a lot of tender loving care, she was able to help a lot of them live when they might have died without it. The day she was sixteen, she got her license to drive the car she had already purchased with the money she'd saved and started working as a bank teller at seventeen. Her work ethic was just like mine, and also like me, her children were by far the most important thing in her life.

Once again, our time together went by in a flash, and all too soon it was time for her to redirect her attention to her family and evening activities. Perhaps we had talked a bit longer than we should have. She gathered Lisa and Lori, told me how much she enjoyed the conversation, and disappeared into her apartment. Once again, I lingered by the pool for a while and thought about the events of the last few days. I realized I felt drawn to this woman as just sitting and talking with her was filling a void in my life I had not previously recognized. I didn't have time to think long on it as I found myself being pulled back into the pool.

During the next six weeks, Jill and I communicated more than we had with our marriage partners in the previous five years. Even though we were interrupted by occasional water games, neither one of us had ever had such deep, meaningful conversations in our lives. We would be in the middle of a topic, and it might be minutes, an hour, a day, or more before we could complete the thought, but we always picked up right where we left off. It was strange to me that even though our upbringings were so different, our conversations revealed how much we thought alike.

Unlike me, she deeply loved and respected her father. At age twenty-one, her dad, Don, was in the Second World War and on patrol when his friend stepped on a land mine. His buddy lost both legs; Don lost his left leg and suffered a lot of damage to the rest of his body. During the year he was recuperating in the hospital, he met Jill's mother, Joyce.

Joyce had been sent by Jill's grandmother to gather some soldiers from the hospital and bring them to a 1946 New Year's party. In less than a year after that New Year's party, Army MP Don, a hunk of a guy with one leg, married a most beautiful girl who gave up the name Turner and became Joyce Kershaw. Jill's sister Pam arrived in mid-1948, and Deborah Jill came in late 1949.

Jill's love and respect for her father was very deep. More than anything, I wanted that with my children. I had no respect for my father, who had abandoned his family, a wife and five children, when I was not yet six. He left my mother to raise my older brother and sister, my two younger brothers, and me in a miner's cabin in the mountains. There were no services—no power, no indoor plumbing, no communication. For eight years until she remarried, Mom raised us by herself. We mostly lived off the land. This most incredible lady was bound and determined to keep her family together.

At the age of ten, I went to work washing dishes at the only restaurant in town. I walked the two miles to work until I saved enough to buy a Cushman scooter for twelve dollars. At age twelve, I traded up for a little two-cycle Harley Davidson. At thirteen, I had an Indian Scout street bike. On my fourteenth birthday, I got a driver's license, and soon thereafter, I bought a Harley-Davidson 61 street machine. After my father left, I determined at a very young age that I would not only take care of myself but also help my mother any way I could. The motorcycles were to become a huge part of the rest of my life.

My relationship with my stepfather, whom Mom married when I was a young teen, had not been warm and fuzzy during the three-plus years I lived with him. I moved out and married my girlfriend when I was seventeen. During the last eleven-plus years, my stepfather and I had developed a deep respect for each other, and in the process, we forged a solid friendship.

My parents and I had spent many days hiking the John Muir Trail in the wilderness area of the High Sierra. They would come to Bishop and Mammoth when I lived there, and we would spend quality time before and after a ten-day backpack trip. Together they became people who taught unconditional love by example.

Jill's dad was always there and was a good provider for his family. When she was a little girl, she carried her dad's artificial leg for him when his stump became too sore or bloody to wear the leg. He went to work every day of his life, often with a painful and bloody stump. He took excellent care of his wife and family and never complained. These were just some of the reasons Jill treasured her father.

She was also very close to her grandmother. This beautiful Latin lady with dark hair and green eyes was indeed a wise woman. Jill's grandmother had three daughters and a son by George Turner. Right after the war, George abandoned his family at about the same time as my father abandoned me. Jill's take was that after a tough time during the Depression and several more years in the navy during the war, almost all of it in a submarine, he could no longer cope with life. On the other hand, Joyce simply saw him as a useless, selfish SOB.

Jill's parents oftentimes spent their Sunday at the Santa Anita racetrack, betting on their favorite horse. Jill went to the races with them as a child, and when she was sixteen, she placed her own bet and won the daily double. No one guessed she was not old enough to make the bet.

Mine was a strict Pentecostal family. My mother remarried when I was thirteen, and both my mother and stepfather—and later my older brother—were to become ministers of God's Word. The chances I would make it to a horse race on Sunday, let alone bet on a horse, were slim to none. My and Jill's lifestyles while we were growing up could not have been more different. My understanding was that most marriages failed because of issues over money, religion, or one of the partners wandering away from the relationship. Jill did not say anything that would lead me to believe any of these were the reason her marriage was in trouble. I did gather that the two of them had never really discussed their long-term goals during the courtship and later found those to be as different as night and day. In my marriage as in hers, we talked to each other but found that real communication was somehow lacking. My mother always told her children, "If you can't say something nice about someone, don't say anything at all." Somewhere along the line, I figured Jill had adopted this philosophy. It seemed to me that she did not feel this relationship was not going to survive in the long term.

After Jill's parents left Southern California and moved to the Village of June Lake, Jill and her husband visited her parents in June Lake and her sister in Reno. Just like us, they thought somehow a new location may help their relationship, so they decided to move. However, it soon became apparent the new location was doing little to help.

When I asked Jill about her mother, she said, "I'll be right back." When she returned, she had a picture of a pretty lady. "This is my mom, and to my way of thinking, she has more class than any lady I have ever met. I love her humor and the way she takes care of my dad. She had a dream of being an actress and gave it up to raise a family. There are a lot of people who give up their dreams to raise a family. I think one can raise a family and live their dreams, don't you?"

"Yes, I think you can. However, I'm afraid that I'm one of those who gave up a dream. My dream was to become an airline pilot, but starting a family got in the way. Getting a commercial license to fly is very expensive. My original plan was to join the US Air Force, learn to fly, and become a commercial pilot. Because all young males were being drafted into the military and there was no war going on, they had more personnel than they needed. They would not accept a married man. That dream went out the window."

We talked about her dreams. Many of them were much like mine. She wanted to visit exotic places, maybe live in those places and get to know people from other cultures. For some reason, Hawaii was a huge draw for both of us, even though neither of us had been there. She had been to Sedona, Arizona, and said the energy there had fed her soul. It was like a different world, and she would like to spend some quality time there. I had determined that living at Lake Tahoe would be a dream for me, and she said that also appealed to her.

Jill's husband would not allow her to talk of her dreams. I, on the other hand, wanted to hear about even her most outrageous dreams. We both felt like we may build a business for ourselves someday. I had invested in two very different business ventures in the past decade, and neither had been a good investment, but not because the businesses were poor enterprises. I had made a bad choice when I formed a partnership. I learned the hard way to be very selective and sure if you're going to be in partnership. Jill had a part-time business selling home interiors. She had a knack for it, and she enjoyed it.

We had both determined we would rather not work for someone else when there was obviously another way, a better way to earn a living.

Everything about Jill was absolutely stunning. She was drop-dead gorgeous outside and just as beautiful inside. She was intelligent, well read, up on current events, deeply spiritual, and just twenty-two years old. Every time I won at the races, there was a trophy girl to kiss, but none was a temptation for me. Jill, on the other hand, fascinated me to the core.

Her questions challenged me. Her philosophy on life was clear and refreshing. Her hopes and dreams were so much like mine. But at the same time, we came from two different worlds. I had been there, but I had never spent any time in the Los Angeles area where she grew up. She had never known anyone who came from the kind of life I had lived, where the basics were not provided and surviving from the land while growing up was a way of life.

For the next few weeks, we spent every weekday afternoon talking by the pool as the kids played in the water. Day after day was like one continual conversation, with one subject always leading to the next. We seemed never to run out of things to share. On the weekend, as couples, we would have dinner in and play card games that lasted till late. Occasionally, we would dine out as a foursome and go dancing afterward. Jill and I had to be careful not to exclude our spouses from conversations.

During all the communication between us by the pool, it became apparent there was something beyond physical attraction. We now knew that we both were unhappily married and that we had known that for some time it was simply a matter of when, not if the marriages would dissolve. The question was this: What would it take to bring about a resolution to the relationships?

CHAPTER 3

THINGS HAPPEN FAST

I knew my marriage was empty and had been for a long time. I knew the pain of having a father leave, so there was no way I would ever let that happen. If need be, I would stay in an empty relationship until my children were grown. LaVon was seven, so in another ten or eleven years, she would go off to college or just move out, and if things did not improve, I would have plenty of time to get into a working relationship.

I immersed myself in my work, my motorcycle racing, and my time with the Baptist church in Bishop. I filled the role of a mentor to young teenage boys at the church. I would take the group camping, sometimes in the high Sierra Mountains, sometimes to the huge sand dunes in Eureka Valley just east of Bishop, where the boys could drive my dune buggy and have the time of their lives. Then there was snow skiing and waterskiing, which not only took a lot of my time but kept my mind occupied.

Jill never did say anything negative about her husband. She said she was aware that she had never really been deeply in love with him. But there was a baby on the way at the time, and she felt there was no way she could ever give up her child. Supporting her child on her own was bound to be a challenge. She felt that a commitment to the marriage, the baby, and time would help. As time went on, she and her husband became more and more distant.

Like me, Jill believed that you should stay in a relationship because you made a commitment—if for no other reason. As with me, they conceived another baby, but that didn't help the situation. There were several trial separations when he would leave for a time, and they would take a break from a stormy encounter. That also did little to help.

Not all that long into this new friendship, we were all out to dinner and dancing at the Comstock Lodge on South Virginia. Late that evening I just happened to be dancing with Jill when the song "Brandy" started playing. The song played, "And so I say Brandy, what a good wife you would be …" This was the first time we held each other, and neither of us wanted to let go. Without saying a word, we agreed. Little did we know just how quickly everything would change.

As I thought about what was taking place in my life from the religious viewpoint I had been raised with, I felt there was a moral issue that I had no idea what to do with. What was going on in my life did not fit well. After all, a married man simply did *not* fall in love with another woman, much less another man's wife. But as most of us know, laws can't legislate the heart.

At the time, I knew nothing of metaphysics, a concept completely inconsistent with my fundamental upbringing. With that perspective, I could have easily ascertained that we had spent lifetimes together and that a previous agreement was simply being fulfilled now. However, that study would not come for many years. From a moral standpoint based on my religious upbringing, I had a dilemma, one that I was unsure about how to resolve. Jill knew what to do.

My wife had Sunday and Monday off, so I did not see Jill at the pool until the following Tuesday afternoon. As I approached and sat by her, she was quiet.

"I can tell something is troubling you. What is it?"

After a moment, she said, "I want you to know you have no obligation. Whatever you do, I want you to be very sure about it.

Yesterday I filed for divorce. Earlier today it was granted. In my mind, if I loved another, I could not stay married. I want you to know that whatever you do, I will be fine. I've known this day was coming for a long time. I simply didn't know what it would take to make me act."

"So how will you support your children?"

"I was granted $75 a month in support for each child, and I just accepted a job at the Golden Venus Spa as a figure consultant. I will be fine."

To put things in perspective, $75 a month was reasonable as rent was about $150, gas 35 cents a gallon, and each bag of food from the store was usually less than $5. One could purchase a pretty nice used car for around $500.

"What about your ex? How is he?"

"He'll be out this weekend, and he'll be fine too. He just doesn't know it yet. Everyone needs and deserves to be loved. He needs to find someone who loves him."

I could tell there was no question in her mind that she knew exactly what she was doing. She did not like doing what she had to do, but she knew she had to do it. She was seven years younger than me, and everything was so clear for her, so cut and dried.

We talked about the events of the summer, the depth of our communication, our friendship, and our attraction for each other. At the end of the conversation, I promised to take some time with my wife and see where she was with it all and what she really wanted. I also agreed at her request not to see Jill or call her until I had resolved it one way or the other. That was one of the hardest commitments I ever made; however, I agreed to it, and in my world, my word was a contract. For the first time since the day we met, there were no words, just a long silence. I knew I couldn't touch her as there would be tears. Sitting there in silence hurt, so I told Jill I would talk to Dottie, find out where her head was at, see what she wanted, and let her know. I gathered my kids and went to our apartment.

"You kids hang out here for a bit. I need to do some work on the bike." I needed any excuse to get some alone time. I had never experienced this particular pain. It really hurt. I left the apartment and a few minutes later found myself stroking one of the most magnificent horses I had ever seen. I pulled his head close to mine just as Jill had the day we met. With that, emotions welled, and tears flowed. But I didn't even care. I realized just how deep my emotions for Jill were. The kids were the only glue that held my marriage together, and this had been the case since some time before LaVon arrived. In my entire married life, I had never met anyone who even interested me, let alone made me feel the way Jill did. On the other hand, I could not imagine my life separated from my children, not even on a part-time basis. I had a number of friends that were divorced and part time dads and none were happy in that role. My teammate and friend Larry Lee was the only one I knew who had kept his kids, Troy Kelly and Cynthia. Nancy had come into his life just recently, but he had spent a few years raising them as a single father. I talked to Larry about it and decided being in an empty relationship with my kids was better than living without them. It was almost unheard of that a father was awarded the children after a separation. Dottie was a good mom, but not so much a good wife. The situation I found myself in left me feeling drained. No decision was not an option now, and any decision I made either way seemed to have no good results for me.

All this took place at the same time our new home was completed and ready for occupancy. It was in Sparks on Norris Drive, close to Reno but on the other side of town. As we were packing, we discussed Jill's actions. My wife said she was aware Jill and I had become close friends and asked if there was anything else to it.

"No," I said, "but I will admit that there is an attraction, not something I understand. There is a deep level of communication. I will not see her again if that is your wish."

She just stood there in the kitchen with a skillet in her hand. I thought she might be considering hitting me with it. She stuffed the pan in a box and said, "You know, this relationship we have could only be described as cordial, and it has been only that for a long time."

"It's true. The children have been the only glue. I'm not sure what to do about that," I said. "I can't live without them."

"I'll have to think about all this. I'll let you know," she said and kept packing. There was a lot of silence during the move.

We had only been in the house a day or two when we sat down to seriously discuss the possibility of divorce. I shouldn't have been surprised, but after thinking on it, she was actually anxious to see it happen. Our biggest challenge would be impacting the children as little as possible. In a short time, we figured out who got what and also agreed that the children would stay with me. She got legal custody, and I got physical custody, at least in the short term since they had just transferred to a new school. I would keep the house because she did not want it. After all, it had no equity. Everything else went with her—everything except the competition motorcycles and the van I used for work and racing and of course, all the bills.

Nevada had very different laws, and in this case, I was a huge fan. If you are a resident and you catch a Nevada judge on the right day and all parties agree, you can get divorced in one day. That is exactly what happened.

We signed the papers, got the decree, and went directly back to the apartment complex we had just moved from, where she signed another lease. During the trip back to the house, she said, "It would be wise not to leave Jill alone for too long. I think she would be good for you, and it won't take her long to find someone else. I know you are good friends, and that's how a relationship should start. That was not how we started out. We had not known each other long enough, and it has been a struggle."

That was it—almost twelve years of marriage dissolved without a harsh word. It was a lot easier than most have it, and I was glad. So I guess our move to Reno worked. We knew things needed to change, and we were looking for a new start. I could not have imagined this turn of events, how it happened, and how sudden it was. I had no idea what the future held, but I was excited to find out.

CHAPTER 4

WHEN IT'S RIGHT, IT'S RIGHT

When I was fourteen, I purchased my first Harley-Davidson, and for the next fifteen years, I spent a great deal of time in the high Sierra Nevada Mountains south of Lake Tahoe. I loved riding fast on the mountain roads. I would park my bike at Carson Pass and hike to the top of Round Top, just south where I could clearly see Mt. Diablo a hundred miles west in the California coast range. I would pack into the wilderness area, sometimes on the main trails and sometime cross country.

Even though I had spent a great deal of time in church, alone in the mountains was where I could really feel and communicate with the presence of God. That relationship with my unseen Father along with my love for motorcycles, the mountains, and the time spent with each is how I dealt with an uneasy home life and troubled relationship during most of my first marriage. I knew these mountains would be a big part of the rest of my life. I needed to know how Jill felt about the things that had become so important to me, so for a first date, I would start with my mountains.

I picked her up in the morning of a beautiful day in northern Nevada. My plan was to head for the mountains. We would just see where the day would take us.

The east end of State Route 88 terminates just south of Carson City, Nevada, at Highway 395 and goes due west, ending in the middle of California, That trans-Sierra route winds through some of the most beautiful scenery in the state. I knew every inch of that road and all the trails that a person could access from it. If this lady did not feel what I did when we got there, I would know that we didn't have as much in common as I had thought. I suggested she layer her clothing and bring not only a swimsuit but also a good jacket as I figured we would know our destination when we found it.

As you cross the Nevada-California state line, you quickly ascend into the High Sierra. Soon you find yourself in Hope Valley, one of three contiguous valleys. The Hope, Faith, and Charity valleys share the Carson River, which winds peacefully through each. At the east end of Hope Valley, the river begins to tumble toward Carson Valley in Nevada, thousands of feet in elevation and miles below. The Faith, Hope, and Charity valleys are absolutely beautiful.

We spent a good portion of this day in Hope Valley, walking by the river, sometimes just sitting and soaking in the sun with air so clear you could see forever. The sky gets very blue at that elevation, and the mountain peaks all around seemed much closer than they actually were. This day the sky was extra blue, and it was a sharp contrast to the various greens of the meadow grass, the pines, the cedars, and the quaking aspen trees. In the background were different shades of gray shale and granite rock that made up the mountains.

The thin mountain air allows the sun to penetrate the skin, and in the cool of that elevation, it felt wonderful. Fresh sheepherder's bread from Bishop and some cheese and veggies along with a bottle of Riunite Lambrusco that we picked up in Carson City made for a perfect lunch with lots of communication, both spoken and unspoken.

As we sat by the river surrounded by wildflowers of every color, schools of trout would watch us from crystal-clear water. Time and again, one of us would start a sentence, and the other would finish it.

We both were ready for a relationship with someone we could really communicate with, something neither of us had ever experienced. We both felt we had found what we were looking for.

We had stopped on the east end of Hope Valley to share lunch, and from there, we could look southwest over Faith and Charity valleys where the highest peaks in that part of the Sierras loom in the background. Jill was at the edge of the river, resting on one elbow, taking in the grandeur of it all. There was a long silence. "The presence of God you spoke of—I get it. It is so strange, but I feel like I have been here before."

"You know, Jill, the first day I met you, I felt I had met you somewhere before. What you are feeling, it's not a feeling one can explain. The feeling you've seen something or someone before and not knowing when or feeling the presence of a spirit that you cannot see—these are things that are hard to explain.

There is something else I feel, I'll put it this way. I have some really good friends in my life, people I can count on. I respect and trust my teammates at the racetrack and some of the carpenters I work with, but I've never had a friendship like this where communication is so easy. You have not been in my life all that long, Jill, but I know in my heart you are already the best friend I've ever had. I just know I can count on you to be there no matter what. It isn't something I believe. It's something I know. It really feels good."

She replied, "I also feel you're a best friend, one I can really count on, and that's the only way a relationship should start. It does really feel to me like I've known you from somewhere before. I absolutely love your mountains, where we are, and how it smells and how it feels."

"I had an idea you would like it here. There are a few things I want you to see before we start back. Kirkwood is the next valley west and is not far from here, and then there's Carson Spur with a huge view of the Sierras and Strawberry Peak to the north. Both are spectacular. But what I really want you to see is Silver Lake with Thunder Mountain as a backdrop. I spent many days there as a kid, sometimes just swimming by myself, sometimes waterskiing with friends from the church. It is an especially pretty area and one of my favorite lakes in the Sierras."

In a short time, we were above Red Lake and over Carson Pass. Then we drove down the mountain to the west, skirted Twin Lakes, and stopped in the Kirkwood Meadows. This was prior to the region changing the name to Caples Lake and before Kirkwood was developed as a ski area. The natural beauty was stunning. From there, we went to Carson Spur, where we got out and took over the expanse of the High Sierra with Strawberry Peak due north.

In a short time, we were on the west side of Silver Lake, looking at Thunder Mountain to the east. The sheer lava cliffs on the west face of Thunder Mountain are best when viewed late in the day with the sun approaching the horizon. They're truly beautiful. These were all places my old Harley street bike had carried me many times over the years, and it always gave me great joy. But I never had the same pleasure I felt sharing this with Jill. While sitting on the west shore of Silver Lake, we were able to articulate how much we loved the mountains and the lakes and what deep love we felt for each other.

The longest day of the year was not long past, so the sun would not set until late in the day. By this time the shadows were getting long, so we headed back. We just caught the sunset over Lake Tahoe, one of the most beautiful places in the world. During a wonderful dinner overlooking the lake, we recapped some of the highlights of our early conversations by the pool. I loved hearing about her most outrageous dreams. It was not only interesting but also gratifying to watch as other gentlemen in the restaurant noticed her beauty— interesting because she seemed oblivious to what was going on and gratifying because she was totally focused on me alone, which was so very different than my life of just a few weeks ago. I liked the way it made me feel.

We headed home and made it as far as the west side of the Truckee Meadows, the valley around Reno. Because Reno is a huge tourist town, it follows that there are a lot of rooms to rent out from one end of the valley to the other. We lucked out in finding a quaint little inn, a B and B on the southwest end. When we set our sails for the return to Reno and to what we thought would be reality, we realized thirty-two hours had passed from the time we had embarked on this little voyage together. It was the most perfect thirty-two hours either one of us could have imagined. Neither one of us had any idea just what we had been missing. If you have never experienced it, you don't miss it. This was a whole new world for both. There was no question for either of us. We were deeply in love. No conversation was necessary.

As I look back, there is not one thing I would have changed, even if I had known this was to be our one and only actual date and that in ten years almost to the day, I would be sitting on a guardrail post up on the Mt. Rose Highway and overlooking this same spot and hurting more than I ever thought one man should or could bear.

Change Is in the Air

By the time I got back to the house in Sparks after my date with Jill, my now ex-wife was totally packed and partially moved back to the apartment complex. It was up to me to move the heavy items. Saturday would be a good time to move the rest of her things.

I was part of a team of young men who raced professional class-A speedway motorcycles, a team we called Check Point. One of my teammates was a guy named Mike, and he agreed to help me move the heavy items from my house back to the apartment complex. After we carried the first load into my ex-wife's apartment, we started for the next load. At that point it occurred to me that Jill had plenty of furniture and everything else we might need and that if we really wanted to know just how our relationship would actually work in the real world, we should set up housekeeping. On each return trip, I picked up Jill's furniture as well as everything else in her apartment and took it back to my house. She was at work so this would not have been the time to discuss it. I was not entirely sure what her response would be, but this way we would discuss what had actually taken place, not what might take place in the future. Looking back, I think I was so crazy in love and not willing to take a chance on losing her that I didn't take the time to think it through.

As I reflect on this, I can see that this was incredibly presumptuous on my part. At the time, I felt I was a practical man, and the trip was from the same apartment complex to the same house. This was going to save a lot of time and effort. My thinking was that through all of our conversations and what we shared on our first date, I knew we had the building blocks of a relationship that only happened once in a lifetime. I felt that I was not willing to live without Jill, and I had no intention of looking any further.

When I married the first time, I was in love, but from the start I always knew something was missing. I just didn't know what it was. We had a child on the way, and I thought somehow his arrival would make it better, maybe cement the relationship. A couple of years passed with little change. Being a mom was all right with her, but she struggled with being a wife. I thought having another child may help. I also wanted a chance at having a daughter and a sister for Abe. My sister was always extremely important to me. I could not have imagined my life without her. We got married very young, and as we grew older, we grew apart. I thought increasing the size of the family would help, but it didn't. As time went on, I came to realize I wanted more than she was capable of giving. She was a very cute lady, and all too often she caught the attention of others. She enjoyed the attention, so I became jealous, which did not help the situation.

What I was feeling for Jill went much deeper, and she returned those feelings. I had never realized that a big part of loving another is having a deep respect for that person. What a huge difference! The communication between us left no doubt in my mind that we could work through the most difficult challenges life could offer. I knew that blending a family would be one of those challenges and had no doubt about her wisdom, which would be crucial to making it all work. For all these reasons, I felt we should start sooner rather than later.

Mike had a younger sister named Tina who was seventeen, and Tina was Jill's babysitter that evening. Tina had felt for a long time she would never understand what made her brother tick. Until tonight, she had no reason to wonder about me. Mike and I had been racing together for several years, and I knew his family well. His father would actually bring the whole family to the races in his motor home. I was about a dozen years older than Tina, and until tonight, I thought she saw me as a pretty sane adult. She didn't think what I was doing was at all right, and she let me know. Things must have looked a lot different from a female perspective. I tried to assure her that I knew what I was doing, but she wasn't buying it.

When Jill got home from work, the only things left in her apartment were a babysitter, two little girls, each holding a pillow and a blanket, and nothing else. In her surprise, she asked Tina, "What happened? Where is everything?"

"My brother Mike and Gabe took it all to Gabe's." Tina helped Jill put the kids in the car. Tina left for home, Jill for Sparks.

When Jill pulled in the drive, I went to meet her. I opened the car door and said, "Please give me a few minutes before you say anything." When she stepped out, I pulled her close, and when she went to open her mouth, I kissed her. I wrapped her in my arms and held her tight for a long time. There was something electric in the embrace. It made the entire body tingle. Neither of us had to say a word. We both felt it.

"We need to get the girls in bed, and we need to talk," she said.

Without saying another word, we tucked in two little angels and watched them sleep for a while. We checked on Abe and LaVon. They both looked innocent as they slept. We walked hand in hand to the living room and settled on the couch. It was time to listen.

She started by saying, "You need to know that had you asked, I would have said no. This is 1972, so we can get away with living together and not much will be said. In our parents' day, this arrangement would not be accepted. I don't know about your parents, but mine will be horrified. Morally, I simply cannot do this. I am not going to be comfortable as a live-in. Even though we have had only one actual date, I also have never been more certain of anything in my life. I didn't think we would have this conversation for some time to come, but you have forced the issue. I need to know what you have in mind."

We spent considerable time talking about what the challenges of having four children would be, how we would blend the family, the fact that she was twenty-two and Abe was eleven, about LaVon and her inability to accept the changes in her life, and any other challenges we might face. I agreed to give up the motocross racing on the weekends, which was not all that hard as I had recently won the most prestigious race in the nation. I still wanted a shot at a championship in Speedway. She felt that was a reasonable compromise. We brought up everything we could think of that would be a problem and how we might solve it.

At the end of a long conversation, I said, "Since you asked, I'll tell you what I have in my mind. I didn't think it would happen this soon, but I want to make you my wife. The day I walked away from you at the pool after I promised not to see you hurt so badly, I couldn't believe it. There was no way I could stop the tears. I didn't even want to. I will love you and take care of you and your children for the rest of time. I know what we have together, and I know how unique and special it is. What I am thinking right now is we need to buy a ring and set a date. Would you stay if we did that?"

That Sunday, we went shopping.

That evening I took a few things to my ex-wife's apartment and told her about our decision. She replied, "I think it's a little soon, but if you really think this will make you happy, you should go for it. You got divorced once, and it didn't hurt you. And that's the worst thing that can happen. I think Jill will be good for you."

We set a date for October 27. Within the next few weeks, we would have to meet each other's families together, try to convince them we knew what we were doing, and make all the arrangements. This was going to be an interesting challenge, and we knew it. We didn't yet know just how interesting or big the challenge would be.

Jill's parents were one of the first problems we faced. Their response on the phone amounted to disowning her, and they did not wish to not speak to either of us. Actually, they had never spoken to me in the first place. They were very upset. It was immediately obvious we would receive no support from them.

Jill's parents were still living in the Village of June Lake, a couple of hours' drive south of Reno. I was up for confronting them, so we drove down. I was not all that surprised when her folks did not want to see me, but the fact that her grandmother was also there and felt the same way stunned me a bit. I figured the fact that this was all happening at warp speed had something to do with their response. Jill's grandmother probably felt Jill was making some of the same mistakes she had made as a young lady.

On the flip side, Jill's sister Pam raised one eyebrow and said, "Welcome to the family. This will be interesting."

I called my mother to tell her. She knew about the divorce, but she did not know about Jill. "She must be really special," she replied. "When can we meet her?" We talked about it, and it did not take long to determine that the best place to meet would be at the Markleeville hot springs pool just east of Hope Valley, a wonderful natural mineral spring about halfway between Reno and Pioneer.

Jill and my parents established what would become a lasting friendship that first afternoon. They would be only too happy to donate their church, and if my oldest brother Rafael could not do the ceremony, one of them would. They made sure Jill knew that they would always consider their grandchildren's mother a daughter and that she would always be welcome at family gatherings. We assured them that would pose no problem. We were all getting along just fine.

Jill's ex-husband had a very different response. It was going to take quite some time for him get over it, but in time he did. We always made sure he was welcome when he came to pick up Lisa and Lori, and he had plenty of time with the girls on a regular basis.

In the next few weeks, Jill would meet my older sister Connie and her husband, Floyd, and their three girls. Connie was a little more than six years older than me and was instrumental in seeing my needs were met from the time I was born until I was ten and she got married. Connie and Jill created an almost instant bond. My brother Rafael and his wife, Marilyn, and their daughter still lived at Swall Meadows, halfway between Bishop and Mammoth, and we drove down to see them.

Marilyn pulled Jill aside and told her that if I had chosen her as a wife, then she considered her a sister. My younger brother Michael, my stepfather's adopted son, was in the navy, but my brothers David and Daniel would come to Tahoe and meet Jill and me for dinner. Every member of my family greeted Jill with open arms and welcomed her to the family. They were all Christians and walked their talk. What a difference.

There was one event that happened while we were living together that had a profound impact on Jill and helped her realize what a huge difference there was between her ex-husband and me and how we each might react to the same event. If this had happened during her first marriage, her husband would have become very upset.

Jill was a good driver and often pushed the limit a bit when it came to getting from point A to point B. This day she entered our driveway just a bit fast, and when she went to hit the brake pedal, she found that her little dog Rags had positioned himself between her foot and the brake pedal. When she hit the garage door, she was still moving at a pretty fair clip. In the early 1970s, we did not have garage doors that rolled up like we do today unless it was a high-end home. As carpenters, we would make the garage door at the same time we framed the house. This door was constructed as a one-piece item that was seven feet tall and sixteen feet wide. It was hinged on each side so that one could pull it up and out. When opened, large springs would help the operator and hold it open in a flat position above the vehicle and out of the way. The single door blew in rather than out as it was designed to do and landed on top of the car, which stopped in the perfect position. The door was held firmly in place by the large springs that normally kept it in the open position and out, not in.

When my framing partner and I pulled up in my van and realized what had happened, we both almost died laughing. We laughed so hard it took a while to open the van door. Once we finally composed ourselves, we grabbed some tools, removed the hinges and hardware that held the big springs, lifted the door off the car, and reinstalled it in the correct position. It didn't take long as part of our job with framing a house was building and installing the garage door.

When Jill told me how her ex would have reacted, I again understood the reason she was so clear when she made the decision to move on.

I turned thirty on October 6, and Jill turned twenty-three on October 16. We were married on the twenty-seventh of that same month. My whole family, a few friends, and members of my parents' church were all in attendance. It was a very special wedding. The most special thing was that my older brother, who performed the wedding, also composed and sang a song for us. Not only did he write the words and the music, but he also played the guitar along with my sister Connie, who played the piano as accompaniment. It was as if the whole thing was inspired. It was the most beautiful love song we had ever heard. The wedding only cost the price of the license, and the only thing that could have made it better would have been if any of Jill's family had attended. Sometime later I asked Rafael if we could record it. He said that it was one of those times when the information came "through him" not "from him" and that he could not do it again, at least not as he had that evening.

At age twenty-three, Jill had not only two young girls of her own but also a new stepdaughter who was only three days away from turning eight and a preadolescent stepson who'd just turned eleven and whose mind worked differently than any she had ever encountered. Blending families is difficult, and we knew the speed at which we moved could have had disastrous effects. Jill's children easily adjusted to these sudden changes in their lives. Lisa and Lori were very young and adaptable. Each of my children reacted differently to what was happening to their family. Abe didn't seem to care that much one way or the other. Racing motorcycles had become a passion for him too. He had just turned eleven, but he had five years of riding under his belt. As long as that part of his life stayed intact, he apparently didn't care about much else. LaVon, on the other hand, at almost eight years old, was not buying any of it. My daughter was not at all ready to share her father with his new wife, who, according to her, took *way* too much of her dad's time. There also were two new sisters who were young and cute and seemed to require constant parental attention. This required of Jill a level of wisdom far beyond her years, but that along with the all-encompassing love we shared made it possible for us to strike a balance. In each case, Jill dealt with the challenge at hand. I knew she was beautiful and intelligent. I was soon going to learn how much common sense and strength she possessed as she took the lead in many challenges we faced. LaVon, our eldest daughter, and Jill would later become the very best of friends. From the day we were married, we had four children. We never used the words *mine* or *yours*. They were all just *our kids*.

CHAPTER 5

A STORYBOOK LIFE BEGINS

The next seven years consisted of storybook event after event as we began to build a life together. I look back with wonder at how charmed our life seemed. This isn't to say we didn't have challenges, but the scales were weighed heavily with blessings.

Shortly after we set up housekeeping, Jill went to work waiting tables at a nice dinner house. She did not leave for work until I was home from my job as a carpenter, so there was little need for a babysitter. The restaurant, which was called Hobo Junction, gave her a uniform to wear that was supposed to depict a peasant girl. It was a really cute outfit on a beautiful girl, and that along with her ability to be very attentive to her customers allowed her to bring home a lot of cash in tips from every shift she worked. With that, she felt very independent, and that was important to her.

The price I was paid to frame each structure allowed me to come home each week with double the amount of the total monthly mortgage on the house. We had a relationship that was more than fun with plenty of discretionary time and money and with jobs we enjoyed. This was a good way to start. Jill's parents could have been more supportive, but other than that, things were going well.

Early in our relationship, Jill led me via California Street to Marsh Street in Reno, which was a very upscale neighborhood. Here together we studied the Tudor architecture she had talked about during our long talks by the pool. I had to admit that the style and craftsmanship of these homes was superb. The high-production homes I had been building in Reno sold for about thirty thousand dollars at that time. The ones in this neighborhood would sell for five to ten times that. It would seem we were a long way off from having one of these. We went back to that neighborhood on occasion to talk about what it was that we liked about each home. I fixed in my mind different aspects of each structure I would incorporate into the one I would someday design and build for the love of my life. My dream was to make her most outrageous dreams come true.

We look back on those days and ask ourselves why it was so good. The success of our relationship defied all logic. After all, a large percentage of second marriages end in yet another divorce, especially those that involve children. What kind of magic had we captured?

If either of us had an uncomfortable issue to discuss, we would wait until the next day or the next time we could sit down and bring it up. Then we could talk about it without emotion. More often than not, by the time we got around to it, it didn't matter anymore. If it was really important, it got resolved without hard feelings. Neither of us needed much space; however, if space were needed, it was honored without question. The more we devoted our lives to each other and our family, the better it got. Were there challenges? You bet. But we tackled each one together, and that made it so much easier.

Little by little, Jill's parents warmed up. I knew it would take some time, but I didn't think it would be such a tedious process. It seemed they would never understand the depth of our relationship. It didn't take all that long for the kids to become just a normal brother and sisters as there was never a distinction in our minds.

Good Things Just Happened

Reno was on the east end of the racing circuit, and neither one of us had a real need to live in Reno. In just less than a year, we made the decision to move to the picturesque Gold Rush town of Nevada City, which was very near Grass Valley, a hundred miles or so west in the verdant Sierra Nevada Mountain foothills in California. Larry Lee, the famed graphic artist, was one of my race teammates and had children about the same ages as ours. Larry's oldest son Troy was destined to become one of the most well-known figures in the moto-sport world. There were others who raced the circuit and also lived there. Nevada City was in the middle of the racing circuit and an extremely beautiful place to live.

Keeping the home in Reno and purchasing another in Nevada City wasn't a problem. The fact that it rained all the time would become a problem though. No wonder it was so beautiful and lush. Much of my carpentry work was outside, and I was missing a lot of work.

We had moved in September, just in time to start the kids in a new school. Just before Christmas, I answered the phone, and a man on the other end of a very long transoceanic wire asked, "Are you Gabe from Reno?"

"My name is Gabe, and I did live in Reno till about three months ago."

"I am a general contractor in Hawaii and I have six hundred units going in Oahu. I need someone to take them plate line up, all truss. You interested?"

"What does it pay?"

"Thirty-five cents. You want it?"

He was asking if I'd like a job framing the roof structures on six hundred apartments in Hawaii. As a carpenter it was my favorite part of building. This was called "working high." Not everyone liked it up there, but I did.

Back in Reno, I had been making about five hundred a week at twelve cents a foot for the same work, and that was big money at that time. Thirty-five cents a foot was huge money.

"I'll have to talk with my wife, but I think I could make it by mid-January."

"Won't do," he said. "I need you to be here right away, or I'll have to find someone else."

During our long talks by the pool, Jill and I had determined that the Hawaiian Islands intrigued us both. At this point the possibility of moving there was not at all out of the question for either of us. However, the call had come on December 15, and I had to be there immediately if I wanted the job. Jill would have to do Christmas with the children by herself. I told him I would call him back shortly. Jill and I talked about the opportunity and how rare it and intriguing it was. I was definitely up to the task. As things were with winter weather in the foothills, earning a living was becoming a problem. We decided to go for it, and if I found that everything was As articulated by the contractor, Jill would bring the children.

I called the man back and told him I would be on board the first flight to the islands that I could find.

A Real Paradise

I loved Hawaii from the time I walked off the United 747 and through the Honolulu Airport. I left the California Mountains in a snowstorm and landed in the tropics. It was 80 degrees Fahrenheit, gentle trade winds were blowing, and the smell of flowers was everywhere.

I picked up a car, drove to the jobsite, And found the man in charge. From where I stood, I could see about fifty foundations. Some had framing going up, and a few were ready for the roof structure. "Can I take a look at your blueprints?" He pulled a set out of his truck and opened them up on the tailgate. What I observed was about as simple to build as anything I had ever encountered. "You told me on the phone these pay thirty-five cents. Did I understand you correctly?" I took the look in his eye to be almost mischievous.

"Thirty-five cents. You up for it?"

"I am. Let me find a place to lay my head tonight, and I will see you in the morning."

He smiled and walked off.

I was told by the crew that the best place to live on Oahu was Kailua Town on the windward side of the island and that I should check with the Kailua Arms Apartments. They had a partially furnished unit I could have in the short term

It didn't take long. I put money down as a deposit to rent a nice home that had a pool. It was on Kaha Street in the Coconut Grove area, one of the more desirable parts of town. The house was just minutes' walk from Kailua Beach, which is one of the most beautiful beaches in the world.

We shared Christmas over the phone and planned the move. It was up to Jill to pack the house, list it for sale, store what she could not sell, and do everything necessary to move four children to Hawaii. As if all this were not enough, more than three feet of snow had fallen, and the Nevada County snowplows had pushed all the snow from the road into a huge pile right in front of our house. Ours was the first house beyond the county road. The propane company could not deliver fuel, and so she ran out. Therefore, the heating system would not operate, and she could not cook. She could not get the car out and ran short on food. Thankfully, a kind neighbor brought food for Jill and the kids and wood for the fireplace and later helped her free the car.

Jill did all this and managed to work in a quick trip to Southern California to bid farewell to friends. She put the wraps on our life in Nevada City and brought the kids and what we needed to set up a house on a rock in the middle of the Pacific Ocean. I was married to a truly amazing woman.

From the time I left for the islands to the time she arrived on Oahu, it was only a matter of a little more than six weeks, but that was the longest separation either one of us had ever experienced. The time apart was something we determined we would never do again if at all possible.

Living on Oahu was perfect for both of us. Everything about Hawaii seemed too good to be true. Though we had a pool, we walked to the beach every day. Right away we met some of the most wonderful people in the world who would eventually become lifelong friends.

Mac and Marilyn were the first couple we met. They also had the kind of relationship Jill and I had. Our new Hawaiian friends were a great deal of fun to be around. We spent a lot of time with them and their friends. All the children were similar in ages to ours, and they all got along. These people only knew Jill and me as a couple and knew nothing of any previous relationships. That along with being 2,500 miles from the mainland and what we thought of as home made our experience here feel like a completely fresh start. We loved everything about our new life—the people, the culture, the food, and even the humid weather.

Just when we thought things were looking perfect, we had our first interesting hitch in our newfound Hawaiian life. The contractor I was working for disappeared. I had been on the job just a few months when we found out he overdrew the job, took all the payroll money, and left the islands. We found out later he took the money and went to Colombia, bought a load of drugs, came back to the US mainland, and sold it to an undercover cop. He got what he deserved.

It wasn't until all that happened that I found out the Honda 750 motorcycle he had loaned me had been turned in as stolen and that he had collected the insurance money. In discussions about all this with other carpenters from the job, one of them said, "Let me take care of it." I had no need for a hot bike, so I agreed. He immediately cut it up, built crates from some jobsite lumber, and shipped all the running gear back to Reno, where he made a chopper out of it. He along with the rest of the crew from the mainland returned home.

Jill did not even want to hear about the motorcycle thing. Can you imagine Jill's response when The contractor's wife, a showgirl from Las Vegas with lots of bolt-on equipment, contacted us and asked if we would show up in court and act as character witnesses for her husband? That was one decision we did not have to think long or hard about.

I had never been out of work in my entire life. I really wanted to stay in Hawaii, but I didn't know anyone in the construction business. For me, this was a major setback.

Nothing seemed to bother Jill. For her, things were never bad, just different. I, on the other hand, was sure that no one in their right mind would ever pay the price I was getting to build, and I saw that as a huge problem. The homes in Reno and Nevada City had not sold, and now we had a third home on Oahu. We had three house payments, six family members to feed, no job, and no contacts. For me, this was a problem. For Jill, not so much.

She casually commented, "I remember seeing another project being built on the ridge above your job the last time I visited. I suggest you just drive up there and find out who is doing it. It couldn't hurt, you know."

I responded with a bit of hope in my voice. "I guess sometimes it's hard to see the forest for the trees. You're right. I'll do it."

I drove up to the jobsite in an old Chevy Nova wagon left by one of the crew who had returned to the mainland. I stopped at the location where the first crew was building, and the whole crew came over to chat. I had never before seen an entire crew stop at once like that. They were all really nice guys and very sociable. Understanding them, however, was a bit of a challenge as they were all native to Hawaii. I had been introduced to Pidgin English, but I had never tried to have an actual conversation with anyone who spoke heavy Pidgin.

"I'm looking for the framing contractor," I said.

"You one carpenter?" the big guy asked.

"Yeah, I'm one carpenter looking for work."

He replied, "I guess maybe one *haole* carpenter okay." I wasn't sure if it was a joke or not or just what he meant. It did not seem to be a term of respect.

"*Da kine*, boss drive one black El Camino. Name Masao." I was told he would be somewhere on the job. I thanked the guy for the information and went to look for the contractor.

I drove around the project until I found a beautiful black El Camino, the driver pouring over paperwork. I stopped my car, got out, and walked over to his vehicle. A Japanese man with a lot of black hair looked up, flashed a big smile, and said, "Howz it?"

"I'm good," I said. "Are you Masao?"

"Japanese name Masao. English name Roy. You one of the haole, was working down on the apartments?"

I still did not know if being called haole was good or bad, but I said, "If you're asking me if I'm a carpenter looking for work, the answer is yes, and yes, I was one of the framers working for the man that disappeared."

He flashed another big smile "You have one crew?"

"Rest of the crew left for the mainland, so I'm a one-man show."

"Each house I have framed by one crew from foundation up. They do it for a price, and I have two carpenters and a laborer on each one. This is the only way we can keep up with the sales demands and I can control my costs. I could use another crew."

I asked him the price he was paying. I couldn't believe it. He was paying the same money per foot as my now missing previous employer had been paying. Then I asked, "If I can come anywhere close to keeping up, are you willing to let me frame the house by myself?"

"One-man show, eh? Frame by yourself? You try then. We see how it goes. How long do you think it will take you to get 1,500 feet of house ready for siding?"

"If it's all the same to you, I will side the walls before I raise them."

"Never seen that done," he said. "We stand walls, build scaffold, and apply siding later. My siding crew will not be happy."

He told me what the siding paid and added that to the price, and we agreed. I could not believe my good fortune. I would have been fine with this first price to include the siding! We shook hands on the deal. Little did I know that that handshake would solidify a friendship and working partnership that would last for many decades.

As I left the jobsite, I had to stop and take in the view in front of me. I was overlooking all of Pearl Harbor, the airport, Honolulu and Diamond Head to the south, and then, Ewa Beach, and the pineapple fields to the north. What an incredibly beautiful panorama. I could hardly wait to tell Jill of our good fortune. When I walked in, I wrapped my arms around her and held her tight. I didn't even have to say anything. We agreed that this was a very good day. No matter how far the pendulum swings one way, it can swing just as far the other.

My first house went up almost as fast as the one framed with a crew, the second one in about the same time as the crew, and the third a bit faster. To be fair, framing with studs back in the early '70s was relatively new to Hawaii. Homes had traditionally been built in a very different fashion called single-wall construction. What was standard for the mainland was very different for these guys. My methodology had been developed over many years, and some of the old boys I had worked with were excellent teachers. You never made a move that didn't count, and many moves counted twice. I was a man with a vision, and this job was going to keep my wife and family in Hawaii. I never took a break except for water, and I would drink one to two gallons a day and sweat every bit of it out. I kept my lunch breaks to fifteen-minute periods, just enough time to eat and catch my breath. At the end of a day, I could look back at a lot of production, and it was very satisfying and very profitable. The local carpenters had a more relaxed approach to their work. We were soon to learn that Hawaiians had more of an easygoing approach to life. The *ohana*, which means "family" in Hawaiian, was all-inclusive where each member was loved, and appreciated. Being part of that felt good to us.

Roy and I were within a few months in age, and we became good friends. I was a master at framing; he was the best finish carpenter I'd ever worked with. He was not only an incredible craftsman and honest as they come in business, but he was also hardworking. He had a wonderful attitude. He constantly whistled a beautiful tune as he worked, and he was one of the most generous men I'd ever met.

To date, we have built many homes and done countless remodels together over the years, and working together is always fun and profitable. Indeed, it is rare to find a partnership that works decade after decade. We've been blessed to have him in our life.

CHAPTER 6

HER MOST OUTRAGEOUS DREAM

I worked with Roy for about a year. The job was lucrative, educational, and fun. Living in Hawaii was good for our family, and we all enjoyed being there. However, we still had two homes on the mainland, a couple of cars, and a lot of things in storage. If we were going to make Hawaii our home, we needed to clean up our stuff on the mainland.

The one thing I did want to do was win a championship at professional class-A speedway racing, something I was close to achieving before we moved to the islands. That was never going to happen in Hawaii as that type of racing only happened on the West Coast. Just a month before I met Jill, I had won the Mammoth motocross, akin to winning the masters. If I was going to retire from professional racing, I wanted to go out on top in speedway racing as well. I was one of the oldest guys on the track with a lot more experience than most, but the kids coming in were just plain crazy and a bit dangerous. Six guys at a time all running bikes fueled with a mixture of alcohol and nitro, throwing the bikes sideways at full throttle into the turns at seventy-plus, all within inches of one another required not only skill but also respect for your competitor. The kids had the guts, but not so much the skill and respect.

We made the decision to go back to the mainland, give me a shot at a championship, sell everything, and then move back to the islands permanently. It took a year, but everything happened just as we wanted. I was able to walk right back into the job I had when I left Reno the first time. There was nothing wrong with the job. We just didn't care for living in Reno. I was on the job one day when Jill stopped by with an Old English sheepdog puppy in the car. He had to be one of the cutest dogs I had ever seen.

"So where did this little guy come from?" I asked.

"He is a thoroughbred that was ordered at a shop in town and never picked up. So I was able to buy him for the balance due. He was still expensive, but too cute, and besides, if we are going to have an English Tudor house one day, we need an English dog to go with it, don't you think?"

"I'll have to say that if we had a home like one of those on Marsh Street, he would fit right in. So what are you going to name him?"

"Sir Sigmund Froyd. We will call him Froyd for short. With all the papers that came with him, he needs to be named after someone smart and famous. So husband of mine, meet your new son. His name is Froyd."

For the next ten or so years, this crazy little (or not so little) dog would be a constant companion for Jill and an unending source of love and entertainment for the whole family. He was to become a big part of our lives.

Focus, Gabe. This is your last chance.

When we left for the islands the second time, it was a lot easier than the first. My division championship was a great way to retire from racing. With homes, the van and all the racing machines, and pretty much everything else sold, we felt really ready to start a whole new life as Hawaiians. We stored a 1967 Chevy Caprice at my parents' house along with a few keepsakes. My parents came to the islands and stayed with us during the first year we were there. My mother and stepfather and other family members promised to visit. We had set it up with Mac and Marilyn to house-sit for them in Kailua while they were in Europe. During that time, we would look for a home to purchase. We loved Oahu, Kailua in particular, and we had a nice group of friends there. We really wanted a home in the Coconut Grove area. When Mac and Marilyn returned from their vacation in Europe, our kids were at their house, and Jill and I were working on the home we purchased right next door.

We knew that Froyd would have to be quarantined so that the vet could observe him for rabies symptoms, but we did not know that would last for four months after he got to the island. That was hard on all of us, including the dog. When we finally got him home to Kaha Street, it soon became evident that the long stay in confinement had been hardest on him. He fell in love with an old bowling ball that had been abandoned by the sellers of the home, pushed the ball all over the yard with his nose, and then mounted the darn thing. He would cry and whine when it got stuck in the foliage. It was strange and embarrassing, especially if friends were over.

I went back to work with Roy. The framing project was complete, but we had plenty of work because he was so well connected. We did new homes, additions, and repair work. It was educational and fun but not as lucrative.

Jill went back to work waiting tables at a really neat restaurant called Rob Roys. The crew she worked with became another group of good friends, and Gil, the manager, was a prince among men.

I looked hard at the possibility of getting my Hawaii contractor's license. But in the business world on that island in the mid-1970s, my round blue eyes were not an asset. As long as I had my friend and partner Masao in my court, I would always have work.

I wanted more than to just have work. I wanted to develop and build my own projects and reap the profits from both construction and sales. I had watched the people I worked for do it, and as I saw it, the only trick to it was getting started. Creating my own construction company would be a good beginning.

After being there another year, we decided it would be a lot easier to start a business on the mainland than in Hawaii. We had also determined a couple of other things. After the second year on the rock, we were experiencing what many called island fever. We wanted to see four seasons and drive for hours in one direction, not to mention the fact that we needed to see family more often. Island fever was not a problem for folks born and raised there. Six round-trip tickets for us to fly to the mainland were expensive. When we put Lisa and Lori on a plane by themselves to go visit their father, it was a big problem for Jill. Her ex came to visit us in Kailua, and that was okay; however, sending two little girls by themselves to the mainland for Christmas was very difficult for Jill. Many of our friends who worked for the airlines could fly wherever and whenever they wanted, so unlike us, they didn't have to deal with island fever and the cost of flying to see family.

Jill and I knew we had several things going for us that should ensure success in the building business. I could build, and she was a natural at decorating. Besides that, we had already bought and sold a couple of homes, and she had an uncanny ability to find a house and make a great deal. She could also make a deal happen when we wished to sell. We wanted to work together, and we felt the housing business would be a perfect way to do that. So we decided to move back to Nevada where all my contacts were and the building business was good. Hawaii would always be part of our lives; however, we would have to build our business on the mainland. Leaving our island home on Kaha Street was bittersweet, but we had a bigger goal.

We returned to Reno, and I got my contractor's license and found my first client to build a new home for. I pulled in contacts from my tract work, did much of the work myself, and had a happy homeowner when I had completed everything. Jill did the accounting, and we made good wages and a nice profit.

When we returned to Reno, we rented a home in the northwest part of town. The home was on acreage and backed up to BLM land. This way, LaVon could have the pony she always wanted. Her first pony was a Shetland named Amigo, and she would ride bareback like the wind, holding on to the mane. He developed the habit of stopping fast and throwing her forward over his head. Her second pony was a Welsh that was larger but just as cantankerous. LaVon became very skilled at riding, and she loved her horses. It was a love we understood.

We returned to Reno since we had contacts there; however, I had never liked the city life, and after Nevada City and Kailua, Jill felt the same.

I had been to Tahoe many times as a kid, and in fact, sometime before 1950, I had decided I would live there one day. One Sunday, Jill and I left Reno and set our course for the Nevada side of the lake. We had no idea that this short trip would have a massive impact on our lives.

The drive over the Mt. Rose Highway was absolutely spectacular. We took our time, stopping along the way just to enjoy the view. Looking back over the Truckee Meadows and the city of Reno was grand, but looking over Lake Tahoe as we dropped down from the Mt. Rose Pass to Incline Village was breathtaking.

The little town and the area around it were pretty, the smell of the pines sweet, and it was also quiet and serene. The Ranchero I was driving had a lot of miles on it, and as luck would have it, the engine died. We rolled to a stop at the corner of Lakeshore and Rubicon Peak Lane. I got out of the car and looked around. The lake immediately to the west was beautiful beyond words. Just to the east and just as stunning to me was a developed tract of land with only a few completed homes. I might not have seen the developed land through all the tall pine trees had the car not quit.

After I looked at the area a bit, I began to analyze the dead engine. There was fuel in the tank, so I popped the hood, pulled a plug wire, and had Jill turn the motor over with the starter. This revealed there was no spark. After a quick check inside the distributor, I found that the set screw had come loose and the points had closed. With the points reset and the hood closed, we were off to do some serious investigating.

Rubicon Peak Lane was the closest street into the developed area. We turned in and found ourselves in the middle of a tract of land with hundreds of tall pines, cedars, and aspen trees. It was completely developed and ready to build on. It was called the Lakeview subdivision. I drove the three blocks to the end of the street and stopped, and then we got out. Jill came around and took my hand, and we started to walk back toward the lake. Jill stopped, did a slow 360, and said, "What a perfect setting for a Tudor home."

"You're right, Jill. That style of architecture would not detract from the beauty of this place one bit." There were a few upscale homes, but it was mostly empty lots. This was a builder's paradise, and we both saw it.

"I'm not sure why the engine quit when it did, but I'm glad it happened now."

She looked at me almost with pity and asked, "Are you ever going to understand how God works? All that religious teaching and you still don't get it."

We got back in the car, drove around a bit, and found signs that directed to the ski hill. All the homes on the hill were built as Swiss chalets. I loved snow skiing and waterskiing, and I could see both from where I was standing. I had already introduced Jill to snow skiing at Mt. Rose, and she loved it now.

"What do you think, Jill?"

"I think living here would feel like heaven to me. By the way, I still think heaven and hell are states of mind. Not so sure about heaven being a *kingdom* or a place where streets are paved with gold that you tell me the Bible speaks of."

"My mom still preaches that. She believes it, and she's looking forward to walking those streets when she dies. Hope it works out for her. I think the last few years have been pretty close to heaven for me. I wouldn't change a thing about our life."

"Me either. Let's do some research on this place and see what opportunities it has to offer."

We had no idea what the real estate market was like in Incline or if the area already had enough contractors. We would try to find a place to rent. If I could not land contracts here, I would be willing to commute the hour or less to Reno if necessary.

With four children, we needed a five-bedroom home. It didn't take Jill long to find just what we were looking for. "For sale, Incline Village, five-bedroom Tyrolean chalet."

Pretty close to 100 percent of our money was invested in our home in Kailua, and for some reason, it had not sold. We called the number in the paper, and a man named Robert answered the phone. We asked if maybe we could rent the home until our house in Hawaii sold. He asked if we had a copy of the listing for our home, and if we did, he wanted to know if we could bring it by his office. We did.

The next day we signed papers and traded the home in Hawaii for a five-bedroom Tyrolean chalet next to the ski lift in Incline—equity for equity, furniture for furniture. We split the closing costs. Robert and his business partner never saw the house in Hawaii prior to closing. For a couple hundred dollars, we moved to one of the prettiest places in the West and into our own home. Our home in Kailua was just two blocks from Kailua Beach, and this home was just two blocks from the ski lift.

The day after moving to Incline, I met a retired contractor from Southern California. He introduced himself simply as Hudson. He was about to bring a couple of homes out of the ground that he planned to sell upon completion. I gave him a price to frame them, and he stuck out his hand. That handshake was our contract. I knew I had quoted a favorable price because I really needed the work. Halfway through the two homes, I realized just how thin my estimate was. No way was I going to even make wages, let alone any profit.

When both were complete, I went to Hudson and asked for final payment. I got my check and was about to leave when old Hudson stopped me.

He said, "Kind of underbid them, did ya?" He knew full well I had underbid the project from the start.

"Yes, I did. Why do you ask?"

"Well, how do you feel about that?"

I smiled and said, "An expensive education, but I'll get over it."

He cocked his head and said, "You're not even the least bit upset at all, are you?"

I shrugged. "No, should I be?"

"You know you did a really good job."

"I know. That's what I do. Thanks."

Hudson thought for a moment and then smiled with a wry twinkle in his eyes.

"I have a proposition. Are you interested?"

"I may be. What do you have in mind?"

"I have fifty more homes on one parcel, and I need them done in eighteen months. I have the dirt and the money. I need a good local contractor with high production experience, one I can trust. I'm not interested in getting a Nevada license at this point in my life. Can you get the manpower?"

"I sure can. What kind of a deal do you have in mind?"

"I'm willing to do a fifty-fifty split on the entire build-out. What do you think?"

I paused a moment for dramatic effect. "I'm up for it. Count me in."

Once again, he held out his hand, and on that handshake I had three million dollars in contract work to execute. There was no way I was going to let the man down, and he knew it. He was one crafty old contractor, and I was going to learn as much as I could from him.

By this time, Jill had the opportunity on more than one occasion to talk with not only Hudson but also his wife, Ginger. When I came home and told her what had just happened, she said, "I had a feeling about him. He is very honest and a very astute businessman, and he has a lot of experience. You are very fortunate."

As it turned out, Jill was correct again. It was to be a long-lasting and mutually beneficial partnership, this time generating millions of dollars all on a handshake.

I knew what the cost was on each of Hudson's spec homes, and I knew what the sales price was. The profits were indeed large. That made me anxious to build my own homes and sell them. Regardless of what the profit might be on a spec home, my general contracting company had about three million dollars' worth of homes to build, and that was going to make it easy to get a loan for working capital to build my own homes to sell. Three million in the 1970s was a great deal of money.

We had enough money to tie up a piece of property, so we contacted a guy named Chuck. We had talked with this man on our way through the Tyrolean Village the first day on our way up to the ski lift. Chuck had the option on a large number of building lots, so we asked him to show us some of his properties. We found five lots we liked that day. They were priced from $9,000 to $25,000 per parcel. We only had enough money to tie up the least expensive one.

We told Chuck we would meet him for lunch at the Hyatt, the only casino in town, and write an offer. On the way into the casino restaurant, Jill picked up a keno ticket and wrote it for a dollar. A regular game was $1.40, but you could play for half of the $25,000 grand prize for just 70 cents, so that's what she did. Plus she played two fours for 15 cents each. The total cost of the ticket was a dollar. An eight spot paid $12,500 if you got them all, and then the two four spots would pay another $1,100.

We were sitting down at the table as the numbers on the board for Jill's game came up.

I wasn't even paying attention to the board. I knew what the odds were on keno, and I thought that the only good thing about the game was it was cheap to play because the odds were worse than winning a lottery.

Before all the numbers hit the board, Jill grabbed me around the neck and squeezed so tight it hurt. When I pulled back, she cried out, "We won! We won!"

Everyone in the place turned to look and see who was screaming and crying. I knew it was good. I just didn't know yet how good.

"How many, Jill? How many?" I asked.

"Eight out of eight," she screamed. "Eight out of eight!" Of the twenty numbers to be drawn, Jill had eight of the first twelve. She won it all—eight out of eight and four out of four twice. Back then a winner was paid 100 percent on the spot and all in cash. When Chuck showed up for lunch, we had a brown paper bag on the table, and in it, there was $13,600 in hundred-dollar bills.

Before we left the casino, we gave Chuck offers on all five lots. By this time, we knew the housing market in Incline had not been affected like the rest of the country. Compared to the rest of the country, we had a good market.

When we got home, I said, "Jill, honey, you won the money. Are you sure this is how you want to spend it?"

She said, "From our first day, this has never been a fifty-fifty deal. You and I from day one have each been 100 percent committed to this relationship, and this is no time to start *mine* or *yours*. I do think, however, we should discuss how we spend our money. I think you should build homes. I'll decorate them, and I'll sell them. While you get the homes going, I'll go to school and get my real estate license. What do you think?"

"Great idea," I said. "You're sure this is what you want to do?"

"I'm very sure. I want to work with you, and I do not want to be a secretary or a bookkeeper."

We both felt we had found what we'd been looking for, not only in a relationship but in business as well.

Our first spec home went on the least expensive lot—$9,000 for the lot and a construction loan of $60,000 to complete the home. I was able to use my subs and suppliers from the big project to build that first spec house. My subcontractors gave us great deals as they had more than fifty other homes they were building for us. Hudson was a master at negotiation and was saving us a great deal of money on materials and subcontracts.

By the time the first spec was complete, Jill had her license to sell real estate. By getting creative, she was able to move the home by trading it for some cash and other real estate that resulted in a net gain of almost $100,000. Part of it was a very low-cost basis. Plus our market was good. By giving three clients what they wanted from this deal and being willing to take some of it over a period of time, it was a win for everyone. Jill was going to be very good at this real estate game.

I wrote contracts to build several homes for other clients as well as one to build a large personal home down on Lakeshore for Hudson. I hired the mother of my foreman on the single family homes as a secretary and bookkeeper. Her name was Marie, and between her and Hudson, we were able to keep track of the cash flow. In just a little more than a year, we completed more than fifty homes. We called our little construction/development company Sundance Development, and it took off as if it were shot out of a cannon.

Jill hung her license with Dave Mays, the man who built the Lakeview subdivision and developed a lot of other property in Incline. Not only did he have a lot of experience at selling real estate, but he was a good man and a great mentor. He took a shine to Jill, and he was going to make sure she was a success. He started passing clients to her, and she found plenty of her own. From shortly after the time she started, she was generating huge commissions. On top of that, the fifty-unit project and other contracts were lucrative beyond anything we could have imagined.

Hudson's daughter Val was also a realtor in town. She had a pocket listing and called Jill about it. We purchased 121 Rubicon Peak Lane, a beautiful building lot exactly where we stood that first day in Incline.

Jill wanted five bedrooms and an English Tudor house in design, but she had no need for anything too large. The plans I drew showed 3,800 hundred square feet of home. But as the cash flow increased, so did the square footage.

What was to become known around town as "the Castle" ended up at almost five thousand square feet with seventeen rooms. This was an English home with five fireplaces, maids' quarters, and a three-story turret. I set up a cabinet and millwork shop, which later became a business in its own right, to do the extensive wood trim inside and out. Every Sunday, there were folks on the street taking pictures.

With almost five thousand square feet, seventeen rooms,
and five fireplaces, Jill had her Tudor home.

The dog Froyd was still very much a part of the family. This Old English sheepdog looked as though he were part of the scene. Early in 1979, another business was presented to us that seemed to me like a good investment. A death in the family of one of our suppliers presented an opportunity to purchase Regional Door and Hardware, the company that was doing a great job supplying a lot of my material. So we bought this door and millwork company in Reno.

Working together, Jill and I covered each other on all fronts— except maybe the home front since running not just one business but several did not leave me much time for family. I could have done better there, but Jill never complained. I was losing my balance when it came to being a husband and father. Being a businessman, which I wasn't, became all-consuming. I was a really good carpenter, but I had little training in the world of business.

Mac and Marilyn from Hawaii along with their family and other friends would come to the Castle and stay with us and ski, but I found myself too busy to enjoy them. I loved the art of negotiating, signing the deal, and making someone's dream a reality. I was responsible for financing and dealing with the county and all their crap. I was too busy making a living to make a life.

Through all this, Jill's parents had come around a bit. They were aware that we were a team in every area of our life and were showing signs of being proud of their daughter once again. But I never felt I was accepted, appreciated, or understood. I had developed a healthy respect for Jill's dad, who he was as a person and what he had been through. We now had a relationship, but it was held at arm's length.

Keeping It in Balance

Now would be a good time to take a look at how we created all this without even knowing what we were doing or just why and how it all came about. Remember, a little more than five years earlier, I was working as a carpenter, and Jill was waiting tables.

After Jill had introduced me to those Tudor homes in that upscale neighborhood in Reno, I focused on one day having one of those homes. I had no idea when, where, or how, but I started designing the home I would one day build for Jill. We made trips to Carmel to the south and Tiburon to the north of San Francisco, and we would find wonderful examples of this architecture in both places. We had even started collecting and storing things that would go in our dream home.

When living in Hawaii, we were at a swap meet at the old Kahala drive-in. There we found a beautiful handmade lamp that would be perfect above the front door of the home that was as yet only a dream in our minds. It had been fashioned by a German craftsman, and it was being sold by his widow. We would one day build our home around this masterpiece.

We had never heard of the law of deliberate creation. All we knew was exactly what we wanted. We never took our eye off the ball and had no doubt whatsoever that it would happen someday. Little did we know we were simply putting into practice a spiritual law that works every time, and you do not even have to know about the law. This law, the law of deliberate creation, simply says, "If you wish to create something, get very clear about what it is you want, hold that vision, watch for the opportunities offered, and proceed in that direction, and it will come to pass." Our charmed life was simply a manifestation of this law. It would be years before we would get into the study of metaphysics and the spiritual laws of the universe. Then we could look back and see how we created this.

The magnitude of the growth of the business and how fast it happened were far beyond anything I could have imagined. I was a humble carpenter one day, and it seemed like the next I was in business as a general contractor with multiple projects in Nevada and Hawaii. I had superintendents on each project, foremen, a crew, secretaries, accountants, and a full roster of subcontractors. Then there were store managers, more assistants, salespeople, and even more crew members.

I had built homes for two of the bankers who had provided funding for the fifty-unit project. Those relationships provided us with capital to work with. We did a spec home with Robert and his partner Mike, the guys with whom we traded the home in Kailua.

A couple of years into this, it seemed as though all I did was answer dumb questions and put out fires. I would give directions and find later I should have saved my breath. This part of the business was a bit overwhelming, and it didn't feel fun anymore. There were too many personalities, and too often most did not seem to have the commitment or willingness to pay attention to detail. Not only did I have the production projects going, but I had nice high-end projects that I could not *piece out*. I had to catch any mistakes my people made. Those mistakes could cost me. This was happening all too often, and it was making me grumpy.

About this time Jill sat me down and said, "This business is making you unhappy. You complain about having to make decisions all day long, directing and redirecting people and having to be in too many places at once. It seems to me that *that* is what a general contractor does. If these people could make the decisions, they would be the general contractor. If you don't like making all the decisions and taking the responsibility, you should give up being the general and go back to working with your tools. From what I remember, you were much happier then."

My wife always had a way of simplifying things for me, getting it out in the open, and articulating it in a way that made me think. It took me a little time to change my mind about my job and to understand my place in this organization. I had to admit that there were aspects of the position that I did enjoy. Negotiating the deal and getting the project out of the ground was fun for me. Getting projects done on time and within budget made for happy clients. This gave me a great sense of satisfaction. The quality of our product was second to none, and this, too, gave me great pleasure.

Then there was the cash flow. A large cash flow is easy to get used to, and I enjoyed that. I never got used to writing huge checks for workers' comp insurance and taxes to the IRS, but I decided the benefits outweighed the negatives. So I decided that Jill was right. I would have to change my mind, be a better communicator, and go for it. I relied on Jill to keep it simple, keep it fun, keep me focused, and generally take care of me in ways I couldn't articulate. We could correct any problems we had by ourselves.

That was the case until the latter part of 1979, when the illness our youngest contracted looked as though it might take her from us. At one point, we were almost sure we were going to watch her die a slow death or live with a serious term illness, meaning that she could have it for the rest of her life, which could have been shorter than normal.

CHAPTER 7

LET THE HARD LESSONS BEGIN

In 1979, our youngest daughter Lori started losing weight. There was no apparent reason; she just kept losing weight. She was only ten, and at first, she seemed healthy enough, just skinny. The local doctor could find nothing wrong. He suggested we give her a milkshake a day and reassured us that she would be fine. But there was no way she could be coaxed to drink even one sip of a milkshake or eat little of anything nourishing. We discovered she had simply stopped eating. She kept losing weight and losing it fast.

While we were watching TV one evening, there was a special on anorexia. The symptoms fit our daughter exactly. At the time, there was little known about anorexia other than that it seemed to affect primarily females in their teens, and no one knew why or what to do about it. Death was not common, but it was the result in some cases. In fact, a very popular young singer had just passed away as a result of the illness. Others lived with it as a term illness, one they would have for the rest of their lives. We had never heard of anorexia nervosa, but we knew for sure this was what we were dealing with.

The next morning we spoke with the local doctor who had just seen Lori. He also had watched the program and agreed that she was anorexic. He would do research and come up with a plan. In the meantime, Jill spent her time at the library in Reno, studying everything she could find on anorexia nervosa, which was defined as the relentless pursuit of excessive thinness. There did not seem to be anything in common among those who were diagnosed except the obsession to be perfect in all ways. And there was no question that our youngest had been the perfect child.

From the time Lori was a newborn baby, she was never demanding. She always seemed content entertaining herself, and as she grew, she always wanted to be her mother's little helper. She finished her chores without coaxing, and she always did her homework before playing. Her room was never a mess. That was really a bit unusual if we thought about it. However, these were all common traits of young girls who became anorexic.

Lori had her mother's olive skin and dark hair. She was a very pretty young lady. When the body is just skin and bones, that person is always cold. In fact, her lips were blue, and she would wear gloves even when it was warm outside. Her body started to grow hair to compensate. There was no way in the world we could coax her to eat anything. Jill's mother came up from Carson City, and supposedly, she intended to show us how we could or should handle the situation. She left as the most frustrated grandmother in the world. We needed help.

The doctor found a team of people in Reno who were studying the disease. One was a medical doctor, and the other was a psychologist. The team met with us and convinced us they knew what they were doing and said they wanted to admit her to a hospital in Reno for treatment and observation. A couple days later when Jill entered her daughter's room, she found her in bed, shaking incessantly. Lori said she had been shaking since the nurse had given her a pill. Jill found the nurse in charge and asked what had been administered. The nurse told her the shaking was a side effect of the drugs the doctor had prescribed.

Jill had not been told about the decision to drug her child, so she simply went back to the room, picked up her daughter, and left the hospital with several people screaming at her, "You can't take her without doctor's orders!" We later determined the *team* knew very little more about anorexia than we did. They simply needed a subject to study and experiment on. Removing her child from the hospital simply felt to Jill like the right thing to do, and it was. As was my habit at the time, I was busy, and Jill was there by herself. When I found out what she had to deal with, I felt really terrible. I should have been there.

In 1979, there was no Internet. Actually, there weren't even personal computers, so research was much more tedious. Jill did find that there were two medical research hospitals in the United States that had actual programs for anorexia. One was in the eastern part of the country, and the other was the Children's Hospital, part of the medical research center at Stanford University in Palo Alto, California. So we made an appointment, packed the family up, and left for Palo Alto.

On the third day of interviews with not only our youngest but all three daughters and ourselves (Abe was on his own by now), the team took Jill and me aside. We were told that they could not admit Lori. Their experience was that if she would not agree to the program and sign a contract to that effect, the program would not work. Each case was unique and included the help of family and friends. In our case, everyone would help except the key member. She had to agree to be part of the program, or nothing we or they did would work. However, she simply would not agree.

At this point we asked what the program would look like if she were to agree. It was a reward/punishment program. According to them, the worst thing for a person with anorexia is isolation and inactivity. We had noticed that she would get up very early and exercise. They would not tolerate this behavior. In the program, if she would gain 0.2 kilograms (a very small fraction of a pound) in weight, she could get out of bed. If she gained again, she could move farther from the bed. As long as she kept gaining 0.2 kilograms a day, she got more privileges. If she stopped gaining or lost weight, her freedom to move would be curtailed.

The trip home to Tahoe was very long and sad. It seemed as though there was nowhere else to turn. There was almost dead silence in the car during the four-hour trip. I was pretty sure Jill would break down if she tried to talk about what had just taken place. I had never seen that, and I did not want to see it now. When we got home, each child went to her own room, and we went to ours.

At first, there were just tears streaming from Jill's eyes. "All I've ever wanted to be was a mom, and I have failed."

"Jill," I said, "you are an excellent mother, a wonderful person, and the best wife a man could ask for. This is not your fault."

"You don't understand. She will die from this disease if something is not done, and no one can do anything. I should have seen this coming." And she completely broke down.

This was one of the hardest things I had ever experienced. I tried to hold her tight, but her sobs were uncontrollable, her body wrenching from emotion. There was no way to console her. All I could do was hold her and let her cry it out. This was going to be a long night. For the first time in her life, Jill had been dealt a blow she could not deal with.

Early in the morning when the sobbing finally subsided, I retreated to the library to pray. I needed help, and I had nowhere else to turn. When the sun came up, it was clear that the only thing we could do was implement the program that Stanford had laid out. I made sure I was right there when Jill opened her eyes. I gave her the most confident smile I could muster and told her, "I have a plan, sweetheart, and I think it will work. We will implement the same program as Stanford would. Are you with me?"

"There isn't much else we can do, is there? I'm with you," she responded.

Implementing the program was easier said than done. The first thing we had to do was keep her from getting out of bed. We felt downright mean. But she had to gain the weight, or she could not move from the bed. Then we had to find a metric scale that would measure in kilograms. It took both of us working together to constantly oversee what seemed like pure torture for a ten-year-old. The more we clamped down, the more obstinate and angry she became. Our beautiful and perfect youngest child was now taking all of the family's time, and it was not fun for anyone. It seemed she was determined to leave the planet and do it in a way that left us all angry with her. It got to the point where her sisters said, "Let her die if that's what she wants to do. This just isn't worth it."

Jill was not only angry with her daughter, but she was frustrated and angry with herself for allowing this to happen. It's so difficult to witness someone you love create that much hell in your life. This situation was the first time Jill had run into something her magic could not fix. I will admit that it was a very perplexing and sad situation.

We were not too many weeks into the program with what seemed to be little success when Lori summoned us to her room. She told us she would do the program at Stanford. I did not know what prompted the change of mind. I could only surmise that she figured she could get by the doctors at the hospital better than she could get by this team at home dedicated to making her life miserable. We were overjoyed by her decision. The restrictions on her were more than she could tolerate, and she let us know. It was a full-time job implementing the program, and it felt like we were dishing out punishment twenty-four hours a day, seven days a week.

So we made the trip to Palo Alto again with the hope that Lori would not change her mind. As ready as we were for the help, leaving her at the hospital was hard. In fact, it was one of the hardest things we had ever done. Being there for each other gave our relationship new depth as if it weren't deep enough already.

For the next few months, weekly trips to Palo Alto were a regular thing. Some of the trips weren't bad; some were heartbreaking. She could have visitors only if she had gained the 0.2 kilograms. There were several times we made the four-hour trip only to be denied a visit with our daughter. Then the return trip would seem much longer. These trips would make for very long, sad days with many hours of driving for nothing. At times it seemed as though we might never see our daughter again as the beautiful, vibrant person she had once been. Other times we feared we might lose her altogether. We felt helpless and sometimes despair.

After she had been at Stanford Children's Hospital for about four months, she gained enough weight to come home on a trial basis. At this point she was able to control her weight within 0.2 kilograms per day, and that is what she did. But she still had very little flesh on her bones.

In 1979, the economy in the United States was still in bad shape. We had a president who had no clue about the world of business or foreign policy and made some very bad political and economic decisions. As a result, the rest of the world started pulling their assets out of the United States, which put our entire country in recession. As usual, the housing industry was the worst hit. You wipe out the housing industry, and much of the rest of the country feels the pain. During this administration somewhere around 70 percent of the builders in the country went bankrupt. The ones who survived did so by reducing overhead, cutting wages (both their own and those of their employees), and learning to live on less. It took more hours to earn less money. Finding the time to work and then spend time in the hospital had become extremely stressful.

Having a daughter with an illness that could be terminal and the extra expenses for that, not to mention everything going on with my business, gave me what I thought was an ulcer. I was doing pretty well dealing with everything outside the family, but the combined stress from that along with my inability to really help Jill was getting to be simply too much. When the pain in my gut would get to a point where I could barely function, I would back off the coffee and drink milk. I simply did not have time to see a doctor. I had never needed to see a doctor in my adult life, and I didn't wish to start now.

Given the circumstance, I was pretty sure I knew what the problem was, and all I had to do was get a handle on the stress.

One night I woke up with such pain in my stomach that I had to bend over with my head touching my knees and I could not straighten my body. Jill took me to the emergency medical clinic in Incline. The diagnosis was a kidney stone. After one shot of morphine, I felt no pain. I was given a little filter to pee through and sent home to watch for the stone.

When the effects of the morphine were gone, the pain was so great that I lost consciousness. Jill ran next door and got our friends Jerry and Penny. Jerry picked me up, put me in his Suburban, and delivered his cargo to the hospital in Reno while Penny kept an eye on the girls.

Without delay, the doctor in the ER diagnosed me with appendicitis. He, of course, could not tell how long I had been in that condition, but he started me on an IV with antibiotics and scheduled me for surgery. Prior to about 1960, a burst appendix, which is what he found, would almost always result in death. Antibiotics had advanced by 1980 to a point where if it was caught early enough, doctors could save about half the people in my condition. If it's not caught early, the odds were not as good. The surgeon found that it had been burst for some time and that peritonitis had set in. That was not a good thing.

He cleaned things up inside as best he could and closed me up. From the scar I still have, I know he did not spend much time closing the incision. For him, spending too much time stitching the incision would have probably been a waste of time given the good possibility he might have to go in again, and if he did, my chances were not good. He told Jill that he thought he got all the infected material but that he couldn't be sure. It was up to my immune system at this point, and it could go either way. He prepped her for the worst.

At the time, there was no way for me to imagine how it felt for Jill to drive home, knowing I was fighting for my life in the hospital while she had children at home she needed to be with. She knew there was nothing she could do for me at the moment. I would be in intensive care for a while. Once home, she got the girls together and told them I would be in the hospital for a while and that I would soon be just fine. She was not about to tell them how critical I was. Then she took Lori to her room.

"Young lady," she said, "I have two people I love very much who are so sick they could die. Your father has done nothing to cause his illness, and I need to be there for him. You are sick because of what you're doing to yourself. I have to be with your father now, so you are going to have to take care of yourself. I can't do it for you."

The next day Jill spent all morning and afternoon just watching me in the ICU. On day two Jill took the girls to see me. I had tubes coming out of every orifice in my body and out the side of my gut. I was hooked up to a lot of machinery, and I was still not coming around. And as far as she knew, I could go either way. At the end of the third day, I opened my eyes and started to respond. In another week, even though I was not in good shape, I was able to go home. My stay was not anything like the months our daughter had spent in the hospital; however, it was too long, and there were too many doctors in our lives. When I got home, I was bedridden for a few days. I could not move my body. I remember looking up and thinking, *This hospital thing has to stop.*

During the time from when I got home until my body could function again, Jill cared for my every need. She was bent on helping me get healthy and keeping me that way. She never ceased to amaze me when she went into action. Not only was she devoted to me as a nurse, but she made sure that the kids had what they needed and that all the chores were done. She worked with my secretary, made the necessary decisions, and signed payroll, and her escrows were still getting closed.

I had missed a lot of work during the time I spent in Palo Alto, and now I was missing more. As bad as the economy was for the country, our town was in better shape than most. Incline was not affected as much as most of the country. Through it all, even though profit was down, we were still making a great deal of money.

In the previous seven years, Lori and I had become about as close as a stepfather and daughter could be. I know my illness had a profound effect on her. I had never been sick a day in my life, and now I was pretty helpless. I made the decision then that I would figure out how this happened and do my best never to let it happen again. It was at this point that Lori started doing better each day, and I figured it had something to do with me and my illness.

Years later I found that Jill's father had also made a most profound impact on our daughter. He and Jill's mom had come to the Castle to be with the kids while I was in the hospital. Like my stepfather, Don was one of the guys who had been through the worst kind of hell in the Second World War. The man never said much, but when he did, it was well thought out. Even with one leg, he was a powerful-looking man. He spent a lot of time walking with a crutch strapped to each arm, and as a result, his upper body was built to take the weight. Through his actions my father-in-law had proven to me over the years what Jill had told me the first day we met, namely that there was deep love and mutual respect between them. He loved his granddaughters with the same intensity.

Lori had been helping her grandmother in the kitchen. She took a little break and found her grandfather in the formal living room, sitting in Dad's favorite chair. She climbed up on his lap and found tears in his eyes. "What's wrong, Grandpa?"

"Lori, honey, do you remember when you were little and you told us your love was so big that it went up to the sky and down to the ground? Well, that is how big my love for you is. I have tears because I can't help you. Nobody can. Only you can help yourself get well." With tear on his cheeks, he told her that it made him sad she was sick, that he was afraid for her, and that there was nothing he could do to help.

For whatever reason, from this time forward, Lori would make her optimum health—mental and physical—a priority in her life.

She does not strive to be healthy. She is health. She learned to keep her life in balance—her body, relationships, family and friends, as well as her goals. It took an illness that brought her close to death for her to make these things priorities. We all need to teach our children from a very young age the lessons learned here. In retrospect, we realized that there was a culture that said you needed to be thin or at least trim, wear the right clothing, and have the right friends in order to be accepted. Jill, her friends, and the other kids worked on this. Being thin was foremost on the agenda for most of the females in that town. Lori took it to an extreme, and it got out of control. Being trim is a good thing, and she will always look that way; however, now she maintains a balance in her life. Nothing is taken to an extreme. The diet is close to the earth. She doesn't overdo it with exercise, and she sets aside time for sleep as needed. This balance is different for different bodies, so you need to find what works for you.

CHAPTER 8

MORE LESSONS

For about the next six months, our lives seemed to get back to some kind of normal. I was back to building, Jill was selling real estate, and the girls were stabilizing. We thought maybe our hospital days were behind us when we had to return to the hospital as our next oldest daughter Lisa (twelve years old) took ill and had to have her gallbladder removed, and again, our attention was focused on yet another family member. Though not life-threatening, this illness was serious and required an immediate operation. It was another setback. It gave us reason to pause and wonder about the illness. Why were hospitals such a big part of our lives? It would be some time before we understood that her diet was the problem. At the time, people focused on being thin. If your diet, exercise program, and mind-set are in balance, a healthy body will follow. We were simply not conscious of that at the time.

It was midwinter in 1982, and the family was again healthy. A year and a half had passed, and things had seemed to settle down. Lori was still controlling her weight, but she was in no danger. Jill and I were both back to our crazy, busy schedules. The door company was losing money; however, the contracting business was holding okay, and Jill's real estate sales never missed a beat. She had worked out a deal with her friend Nancy, one of the other ladies in her office, in which they would take care of one another's escrows and clients if one or the other was absent. Her real estate business continued to be very lucrative and rewarding.

However, just as we were beginning to relax into life, crisis hit again. Through all of the hospital craziness from mid-1979 to early '82, LaVon was coping and taking care of herself just fine. So when the call came to meet her ski coach at the hospital, somehow I was not surprised. It was now her turn. Competitive skiing had become a big part of her life. She had started at a young age and had become very skilled. She started competing in grade school, and since joining the Incline High School ski team, she had spent about a hundred days a year on the slopes, a good deal of it under instruction. She and her friends would free-ski or ski the back country on the weekends. Outrunning an avalanche was about the most fun she could have. It would seem that both of us loved an adrenaline rush.

When I got the call from her ski coach, he simply told me that I should meet him at the hospital and that LaVon was being transported by ambulance. As I was driving to the hospital, I thought about LaVon's friend and teammate Mark Fisher, an excellent skier who had died on the slope at Squaw a couple of years earlier. He was just a young teen, and I could not fathom the pain and loss his parents had to endure. LaVon had to be okay. She just had to be.

In training or during a race, missing a gate or losing control during a run was not common, but it happened. One had to ski to the limit to win, and the only way to know your limit was to test it. Fearless, LaVon tested her limits often. This was the first time in some ten years of skiing and racing that she did not get up after she went down. When I arrived, I met her coach in the waiting room. He did not have any kind of a report from the doctor, but he suspected a neck injury as she could not move her head or upper body and she was in a great deal of pain. I did not want to call Jill until we knew what we were dealing with.

As I sat in the waiting room, I thought about what LaVon meant to me. We had always been very close, and she had accepted Jill as her mom. They also had become very close. She did not seem to encounter the normal challenges so many girls did when becoming a young adult. She had none of the classic self-esteem issues. She was popular, pretty, and athletic, and she had a great sense of humor. I simply could not think about her being badly injured. Once again, I found myself in another hospital waiting room, and I didn't want Jill to endure any more of this if she didn't have to. Neither the coach nor I had to say anything. We both knew what a special young lady LaVon was. When the doctor finally appeared, we both jumped to our feet.

"Okay, Doc, I need to know everything you know. What are we looking at?"

It was a really good report, given the circumstances.

"LaVon has dislocated her collarbone, which is very painful, immobilizing the upper body, but not hard to correct. I have put things back in place. She will be very sore for a while. She needs to keep the shoulder immobilized for a couple of weeks and then take it easy for some time. She is young and healthy, and she will be just fine. But she won't be racing for a while."

I called Jill at her office and told her where I was and what had happened. "I'll be right there," she said.

"No need, sweetheart. I'll bring her home when she is discharged. She'll need help for a week or so. You'll have plenty to do then."

Within minutes Jill was at my side. She was going to be there for me and be there for our daughter.

When we got home, we found that Lisa had been riding the lift up just above the race course and had seen her sister take the fall. She said she knew it was a bad fall and was ready to bail off the lift chair when she realized she was at least two stories up. By the time she got to the top of the mountain and skied down to where the accident was, the ski patrol had her sister on a stretcher and were heading for the ambulance. She was not allowed to go with her sister and had to go home and wait for news. She realized how much she cared for her sister and how devastated she would be if she were hurt badly. It was a long afternoon for Lisa.

It wasn't long before LaVon was on the mountain again, arm in a sling, keeping her legs in shape and looking forward to the next race. More than three decades later, I still worry about our eldest daughter from time to time. She's still on the ski hill at least a hundred days a year, pushing the limits, catching an adrenaline rush. Sometimes some of those days are in the Alps in Europe or in Alaska, often in the US or Canadian Rockies, high above any ski lifts. In between these trips, she is in the High Sierra above Tahoe.

CHAPTER 9

TIME TO REFLECT A BIT

By the spring of 1982, normal life had returned to the Castle. The door company and the cabinet shop were paying their way, and the construction company and Jill's real estate business were doing fine. One of the upscale homes under construction was for a client who was the president of a large savings and loan company. It had taken a couple of years from the time the contract was signed to the time design was complete and permits were pulled. The owner and I had worked on all that together, and we had established not only a working relationship but a friendship as well. At the time I had no idea what a huge part of my life (our lives) this man would become.

Ronald Reagan had been elected president and had made some bold moves. In spite of a congress that simply did not seem to understand things, the economic picture, at least on the horizon, was looking up. The last few years had been difficult, and I was looking forward to a productive and enjoyable summer. I was anticipating spending more quality time with my family, especially my wife.

The spring months of April and May were simply beautiful at Tahoe, and I had time to reflect on the past nine or so years. We had accomplished some things that were unbelievable, and on the flip side, things had happened that were truly devastating. We had envisioned the amazing things we accomplished almost ten years earlier. But I needed to figure out why we experienced the illnesses and setbacks.

Why all the hospitals? Maybe sometime in the future, I could look back on it all and figure out what we had done to create that. By this time, I knew that by creating a mental picture of what we wished to see happen in our lives and holding on to the vision, we could manifest what we wanted. I just did not know how we might create what we *do not* want in our lives. How and why we might do that made no sense to me. It would be years in the future before we understood that for the growth of the soul, things come into our lives that don't seem in our best interest. Maybe we set something in motion, and the results may seem bad or at least really uncomfortable. Sometimes bad things just happen. How you react determines whether or not the situation becomes a positive or a negative.

Life Moves On

Snow skiing was something Jill had taken an interest in, and she had become a great deal of fun to ski with. The fun didn't stop in winter though. The Castle was just a couple of blocks from the lake, and launching the ski boat in the summer took only a few minutes. There was a huge private beach for the residents, with a boat launch, lots of sand, tables, and barbecues. People were always playing volleyball games. It was a great place to gather with friends and family. Many of the people we knew had ski boats, and waterskiing was a big part of life for our family life.

Just how the ski boat came into our lives is a story in itself. Back in 1976, we had traded our home on Oahu for the first home in Incline. Robert and his business partner, Mike had subsequently asked Jill and me to join them, their wives, and some friends for a weekend on a houseboat on Lake Oroville. They would be there from Thursday through Sunday. As Jill and I could not make it until

Friday afternoon, Robert agreed to pick us up at the marina with his ski boat. It didn't take me long to realize what an exceptional boat this was. It was a beautiful, sleek powder blue jet boat with the largest engine Ford ever made.

As I hadn't ever heard of the make before, I asked Robert where he got it. He said the design was copied from a major line, and now the company that made his boat was no longer in business. He said they didn't simply copy the design but improved it substantially; however, they had not changed things enough to win a copyright infringement case in court. They lost, and this boat was the last one they ever made. I asked if he would be interested in selling it. He said no, but he also told me that that if and when he ever did want to sell, I would be the first one he called. The weekend was *very* different than we expected.

As we pulled up to the houseboat, we first noticed how secluded we were. The next thing we noticed was that none of the ladies had tops on. He never mentioned this topless thing at all. He hadn't even hinted at it. Everyone seemed comfortable except us. Remember, this is in the mid-1970s, and a lot of people had been hippies and flower children in the '60s. As a result, this behavior did not seem to be much of a stretch for them. For us, though, it was. I was not all that comfortable with the program, but Jill was downright uncomfortable.

Some polite discussion ensued about how we were feeling about everything, and they assured us that they had a solution that would help with the comfort level. Jill and I knew little to nothing about drugs of any kind, even pot. We were assured that after one puff and a long inhale, we would be just fine. After giving it a shot, we became more "relaxed" about the issue. I remember sitting on the boat and saying, "This doesn't bother me at all." Trouble was that I was saying it over and over and could not seem to stop. Everyone was having a great time at my expense. As promised, the pot did help with my comfort level. The substance helped Jill only to a point, and that point was just short of removing her top. She simply could not go there. As the effects wore off, we determined that even though it helped with how we felt about the situation we found ourselves in, the "out of control" feeling was not something either of us liked.

A couple of years later, Robert called. He said that he was moving to Carmel-by-the-Sea and that the blue boat was not made for the ocean. "You still interested?"

I said, "You want cash, or is a check okay?"

That day we owned the perfect Tahoe ski boat. We spent a great deal of time in that little jet boat. If we weren't skiing, we were going to Emerald Bay for a picnic or sometimes to South Shore, just hugging one shore down and the other back. The fact that it was a jet allowed the craft to skim over huge granite boulders that were close to the water's surface.

The water in the lake is so clear one can see the Indian head on a nickel twenty feet below the surface. As such it was hard to judge just how close big granite rocks were from the surface of the water. No one ever got tired of spending time on the lake. There were times in the spring when we could snow ski in the morning and go to the beach in the afternoon. From May through September, the family spent a lot of time at the beach and a lot of time waterskiing.

It was late in May 1982 and nice enough weather to take the boat across the lake to a restaurant on the west shore called Sunnyside. The place had a beautiful deck overlooking its dock and the lake, and we would have brunch there on occasion. That day I would endeavor to ski the twelve or thirteen miles across. What I did not figure on was how choppy the water got in the middle of the lake. I was skiing fast, and as a result, when I lost it, I hit the water hard. I'm not sure just how it happened, but somehow my left arm was wrapped around the ski when I went in. This injury to my shoulder caused pain whenever I used my arm.

I was familiar with the type of injury. I knew a doctor would take an X-ray, recommend I favor the arm, and see if it would heal. If it did not, he would want to schedule surgery. At this time in my life, I was done with doctors and wanted no part of hospitals. The arm was slow to heal but doing much better. Then the following winter, I was on the ski hill, did a major face-plant, and tore the shoulder again. This time it hurt even worse, but I was still not going to see a doctor. At the time, I knew nothing of holistic or spiritual healers, and I had no idea this shoulder injury would later become a big part of our story.

And all through this, the questions remained in my mind. *Why all the hospitals? Why all the illness and injury?*

Little did I know that our biggest test, one that would shake the family to the core, was just around the corner.

CHAPTER 10

THE LONELIEST
ROAD HOME

It was early in the morning of June 2, 1982. Jill was not only helping the girls get ready for school, but she was also getting ready for her weekly MLS meeting as we called it with all the realtors in town. As with many townships, the real estate business has an organization of all realtors in town where a real estate salesperson could find all the property listed for sale. They ran was call their "Multiple Listing Service. Each week all the realtors would gather at one place and share information with regards to the business of buying and selling.

With a husband, three teenage daughters, and a full-time job in real estate, not to mention a huge house to maintain and an active social life, she was a busy lady. Our lifestyle required her to move quickly from task to task all day.

As she seemed a bit slower than her usual self, I asked, "Jill, do you feel okay?"

She said, "I'm okay. Just feel a little tired this morning. I'll be fine. Remember, I won't be home till late tonight. Mom and Dad and I are going to take Pam bowling this evening at the MGM Grand and then out to dinner to celebrate. It's my sister's birthday, remember?"

"I remember. You have a good time. This will be an opportunity for me to spend some time with the girls. I'll see you when you get home tonight."

Reno is more than a half-hour drive to the east of Incline and over the summit at Mt. Rose. The pass is high, and the road narrow with many tight turns. Driving over the pass to Reno was simply called "going over the hill," and we drove that route often. Late in the evening, the phone rang. It was Jill.

"I kind of expected you home by now," I said. "What's going on?"

"I feel too tired to drive back over the hill and think it best if I stay with Pam tonight. I'll see you in the morning."

It kind of sounded as if she had consumed one too many glasses of wine, which was not at all her style. The Mt. Rose Pass was no place for anyone to drive who was tired or tipsy.

"Okay, sweetheart, sleep well, I'll see you in the morning. Make it early though. I have a heavy schedule tomorrow."

As I crawled into bed alone, I thought about how lucky I was that Jill was there 99 percent of the time. In almost ten years, we had not spent many nights apart. I never liked it when it happened, but for some reason, I felt especially uncomfortable about it this night. As was my habit, I prayed before sleep. I thanked God for this incredible lady who completed my life. I thanked him for the key role she played in raising my children. My sleep was restless that night as I had a nagging feeling I could not put my finger on.

I called Pam's house in the morning, and Jill answered. She sounded as if I had roused her from a deep sleep, and she was not coming back into her body all that fast. Her sister had already left for work. We could not agree on a place to meet for breakfast, but we did agree she would call me in my car after she showered and dressed and got her head clear. I had meetings in Reno all day, so I headed toward Pam's apartment. The call from Jill never came, and when I reached Pam's house, there was no answer.

I assumed Jill had gone back over the hill as she had several properties in escrow, and if they were too close escrow on time, she needed to pay attention to each of them.

I could not call her, as cell phones had not been invented yet. The phone I had in my car was a radio phone, which was large and permanently mounted, and it had cost almost as much as the car I was driving. When I picked up the handset and pushed a button, an operator answered. I asked her to connect me with my home, but there was no answer. The operator then tried Jill's office, but she wasn't there either. The past ten years had proven Jill was more than capable of taking care of herself. I'd find out what happened when I got home tonight.

I had several important appointments scheduled that day, and everything seemed to be going well. As I often did, I would make the last stop of a day in Reno at Regional Door and Hardware. When I entered the office, I received the news that would change my life forever.

The next thing I knew I was sitting on a guardrail post at the eight-thousand-foot level on the Mt. Rose Highway, hoping I would wake up and all this would be a bad dream. I sat there for a long time, looking over the Truckee Meadows. It had all started at the bed and breakfast just south of there almost ten years earlier, not far north my beautiful wife lay in the hospital with an unknown amount of damage to her brain. I felt numb, almost paralyzed. I didn't want to move. Had I known the true extent of the hell I would face, I don't know how I would have reacted. This was the third day of June, and even at eight thousand feet in elevation, it was not too cold. I just sat there for a long time.

When I finally made it back home, there was not enough time to do anything but take a shower. So I spent the rest of the time I had left of the night in the library, praying.

I do not remember what I told the girls when they got up, but this was the first time any of them had seen their dad with swollen red eyes, so I am sure they knew it was not good. After school I would take them to see their mother at the hospital. None of us could have guessed this would become part of our routine for the rest of the year and well into the next.

CHAPTER 11

THE NIGHTMARE CONTINUES

Early that morning I called some of my staff and had them meet Marie and me in the office. I explained to them what had happened and what we knew so far, and I also told them that at least in the short term, they would have to assume some additional responsibilities. I could not stick around until the bank opened for the deposit, so one of them would have to take care of that for me. I called Jill's office, and Nancy answered. I told her what had happened and also said that I would keep her informed as it all unfolded. I delegated the rest of my day and left for the hospital.

Until now my experience with the medical profession had been positive for the most part. The people who had taken Lori to study and started administrating drugs were working at this same hospital. That was the first time we had ever questioned the Western medical profession. But these people should have known something about a stroke. Once I got to my car, it didn't take long to get to the hospital.

When I entered Jill's room, she didn't respond. I kissed her head and asked her, "How do you feel?"

She opened her right eye. "Left eye ... can't focus on anything. Left arm and leg ... hard to move them."

The left side of her face just wasn't right. It seemed to sag. Her speech was slurred. Once again, I was not able to remove my emotions from the situation. Shortly after that, a nurse came in and said, "It is time for another test, young lady. We need to know what is going on here."

"Can I stay with her?"

"Not for this one. We will be in an operating room."

"Operating room? What kind of test?"

"Your doctor wants a cardiologist to look at her heart from the inside. Don't worry. No one is going to cut her open. It is a pretty noninvasive procedure, and we do it all the time."

"How long will it take?"

"No too long. Why don't you get some coffee or something in the cafeteria? Someone will come and get you."

I got a cup, sat down at a corner table, and watched people from all walks of life go about their business—some serving others, some medical staff, others waiting it out just like me.

It was not long before Joanne came in. She walked straight to me and held out her arms. Jill had a lot of friends in Incline, and Joanne was one of her closest. After a short embrace, she pulled back. "Nancy called me. What's going on? How is she?"

"Not good. She is having a test run right now. Grab a cup or something, and sit down. I'll tell you what I know."

Little did I know that I would share this table with Joanne and many other friends and family members for months to come.

They threaded a tiny camera through a large vein from her leg to her heart. It revealed a shunt—a hole in her heart. If the body is working properly, blood is pumped from the right side of the heart and through the lungs, where it is filtered and picks up oxygen. Then it goes to the left side of the heart, where it is pumped throughout the body. The clot had apparently traveled through the shunt from the right side of the heart to the left without going through the lungs as it would normally. The neurologist surmised that the surgical procedure on her foot must have created the clot. Then the clot made it to her brain, where the vein burst. We now understood that no surgery was ever minor, even one to simply remove a bunion. Any invasive procedure comes with significant risk.

She kept losing function on the left side of her body. The neurologist seemed to me a bit detached about the gravity of Jill's condition. On day three in the hospital, I cornered him.

"Doc, my wife is getting worse every day, not better. What the hell is going on?"

"It's the evolution of a stroke," he said. "We will just have to watch and see where it goes. It is my hope that when she stabilizes, she has enough left to undergo open-heart surgery."

Day after day, Jill's condition grew worse. In 1982, much less was known about strokes. At that time, many believed that unless the brain was treated within twenty-four hours of the onset of the attack, little could be done to prevent the subsequent tidal wave of damage and symptoms. But through research, much of that thinking has now changed. Today much physical devastation could have been prevented. While it's still imperative that treatment be given as soon as possible, the types of treatment have expanded, giving today's stroke victims a much clearer path to recovery. Unfortunately, people didn't know this information then.

After a week and a half in the hospital, Jill seemed to stabilize. After few more days, the doctor would release her so that we could take her home. The hope was she would gain enough strength in a month or so to survive surgery to close the hole in her heart. Her left leg and arm were almost useless. The left side of her face sagged, and her speech was slurred. That is how I took her home.

At that point, her doctors were doing all they could. She was on blood thinners to alleviate the chance of another stroke. While at home, we would go to the clinic in Incline every day and do a blood test to make sure her blood was thin enough. The medical team researched the best forms of treatment and sought the finest surgeons and facilities that would offer her the best hope for healing and recovery. They recommended Cedars-Sinai Medical Center in

Hollywood. There she would get the best treatment possible. That hospital had the best reputation in the nation for open-heart surgery successes at the time. I went with this recommendation, so she was scheduled to have the procedure done in Hollywood in a little more than four weeks.

It was heartwarming to watch Jill's friends come in shifts to help her. They fixed her hair, did her makeup, and helped her do what the physical therapist had recommended. I remember watching Penny from next door trying to stabilize Jill as they walked up Rubicon to exactly the spot where Jill had stood years earlier and visualized the home that now stood there. Something was very wrong with the whole picture. I would have given up the Castle in a heartbeat to make Jill healthy again. With all the help Jill was getting, I still could not pay attention to my business life. Looking for new work was out of the question. I had enough trouble dealing with the homes that were already out of the ground. I was lucky that I had developed good crews, subcontractors, and office personnel. My part was dealing with the owners, bankers, architects, and county officials. I usually had the luxury of stepping back from a challenging construction task and figuring out the best way to accomplish it. Normally, the bigger the challenge, the better I liked it. Facing this new challenge at home was about all I could handle.

At seventeen years old, LaVon just stepped up and started filling some of her Mom's roles. I didn't know at the time that Joanne had been spending a lot of time not only with Jill and me but with LaVon too, talking about what she could do to take some of the load off me, including some of the things a mom usually did. She did meal planning, shopping, and family laundry, and she saw to it that her younger sisters were where they needed to be when they needed. She went to school full-time, worked a part-time job at a restaurant in the evening, helped run the household, and worked in a bit of time with friends at the beach. She had developed an unusually close relationship with her stepmother, and she watched her closely in action. She said, "If Mom can do it, I can do it." And she did.

Lori and Lisa were twelve and thirteen at the time. Kids at that age can be pretty self-absorbed. The physical therapist had laid out things for Jill to do to regain her eye-hand coordination, things like puzzles and toys you usually give to toddlers or very young children. Jill's friends would spend time on the floor in the den and work with her. That scene just didn't work for the girls. They did what they could to keep themselves busy. They just didn't want to think about what was going on with their mother.

From Bad to Worse

Getting out of a water bed was a challenge even if your body was working properly. This was more of a challenge than normal for Jill.

Jill could get to the edge of the bed, where I would support her, but she needed help to get from there to the bathroom. Just days before we were scheduled for the heart surgery, Jill got to the edge of the bed and collapsed on the floor. She could now no longer use the *right* side of her body.

I picked her up and carried her to the bathroom. That did not work either. I carried her to the car, reclined the seat because she could not sit up, and headed for the hospital in Reno. On the way over the hill, I called the doctor and explained that while Jill could stand up the previous night before bed, she could not stand this morning. He said he would meet us at the hospital.

The initial diagnosis was another stroke, this time in the left hemisphere of the brain, which affected the right side of her body. *This just can't be,* I thought. *The left half of her body was not working well at all. And now the right side?*

There was no wheelchair this time. She was moved on a gurney. While I was getting Jill admitted again, I just felt numb. This was *not* going in a good direction. By the time I got to her room, she had been rolled in and transferred. She was scheduled for more tests, which was not what I wanted for her.

Yesterday her speech was slurred, and she was hard to understand. Today she was even worse.

Jill had confessed to me that during the first go-around when they pumped dye into her veins to watch it travel through her brain, it felt like molten lava in her head. The pain was so severe that if they ever wanted to do that again and the only other option was death, she would rather choose death. But *damn it all,* they convinced me to okay the procedure again. They said if they were going to help her live, she *had* to endure the test.

This time when I carried Jill to the car and then into the hospital, she was completely limp, and she didn't have a single muscle reaction. I felt helpless, and the fear of losing my beautiful wife meant that I would do whatever they told me to do if it meant saving her. I had no idea at the time they were simply grasping at straws.

The results of the scan showed nothing remarkable. There were more tests, and Jill's condition grew worse. None of the testing was adding up. By the end of the second week, Jill could barely make a sound. Another week passed with less movement and less response. Now every day she was slipping away. With every test she could move less and respond less, and she was losing her sight. Her body was shutting down day after day. This went on week after week. June passed. It was now mid-July. The nightmare just kept getting worse.

Each day I would enter Jill's hospital room and realize she had less to work with than the day before, and I would feel an overwhelming sense of despair, helplessness, and profound sadness. I was losing confidence in the doctors and felt I had nowhere else to turn.

We had always told each other everything. We shared our most intimate feelings. Now I didn't want her to know what I was feeling, and that did not feel good.

I would get close and tell her, "Honey, I'll be here until the end of time if that's what it takes. I'll find an answer." I had no idea whether she could hear me or not, but it made me feel better to say it. The doctors talked to me *about* her, never *to* her. They acted as if she were already gone. That did not feel good either.

I couldn't give my business life what it required, but it seemed to function at some level. As far as I could tell, the girls were coping better than I was, and right beside Jill was the only place I wanted to be. Friends would come and go, but as time went on, that happened on a less frequent basis. Jill's good friend Joanne had been there for us from the onset, helping me with the girls and at the hospital with Jill. At first she would do Jill's nails, which would help Jill feel normal. She would spend time with me over a meal and just listen. My good friend Dick, her husband, took care of the domestic chores and their children so that his wife could be there for us.

In years past, Dick, Joanne, Jill, and I would load up our kids and drive to Ketchum, Idaho, which was fourteen or fifteen hours east of Incline, to spend a week skiing the huge mountain at Sun Valley, where the powder was some of the best in the world. This is where skiing deep powder became an addiction for our daughter LaVon.

As Jill's condition became more and more like that of a vegetable, the situation must have been more than Joanne could deal with. One day I found myself totally alone.

Other than Jill's parents, I was pretty alone in her room most of the time. There were thirty-six patients on her floor and six nurses. With the paperwork required, the staff had little time to be with each patient. Jill could not respond, but she could breathe on her own, so her care was pretty much left up to me, her parents, and the private nurse I had hired to be there when we could not.

My sister Connie and Jill were very close. She and her husband, Floyd, made the two-and-a-half-hour drive from Pioneer to see Jill. Connie later told me it was a couple of days before she and Floyd could even talk about their hospital visit. They were both in shock, feeling inconsolable grief. How had this happened to our beautiful Jill? She was far too young for us to lose her this way. We were all asking that question.

I hired a lady to be there for the girls. The house had a full one-bedroom maid's apartment, where she stayed. I stayed with Jill at least eight hours a day. Jill's parents took a shift, and I hired a nurse from a private agency to be with her the balance of the twenty-four-hour period. Betty, the private nurse, talked to Jill and took care of her every need. She would talk to Jill and treat her as if she mattered, touch her, and read to her. The staff simply did not have time to even help feed Jill. I did not want her to be alone. I felt with every cell in my body that someone who loved her needed to be by her side at all times if she were going to survive.

I did not know at the time, but because Jill would cry when friends came, her mother had asked folks not to come. Her crying was not audible, but the tears would flow anyway.

No Good Answers

In August, about a dozen mystified doctors were still looking for answers. One of them came up with the idea that they should test for multiple sclerosis. I remember the doctor saying that he took a generous amount of spinal fluid, which is what they used for this test. At that point, I had no idea that the brain was normally insulated from the skull by spinal fluid and that the correct way to go about this test was to take as little as possible. When the brain no longer has that cushion, it rests against the skull, resulting in an incredible amount of pain. The doctor should have known that.

Percodan (a heavy-duty painkiller and muscle relaxer) was the drug this doctor prescribed, and Jill was already on blood thinners. I had no idea how dangerous this combination was and would not find out until much later. This doctor and the staff should have known better.

On top of the pain she felt, Jill was frustrated that she was unable to communicate, feeling abandoned by her friends and battling overwhelming fear and uncertainty. Her tears never stopped.

We believed Jill's pain was gone; we knew for sure she couldn't move at all. With the excellent communication we'd always had, we often knew what the other was thinking before we said it. I brought my face close to hers and said, "Honey, if you can understand anything I say, just blink once." She gave no response, nothing at all. Little did I know she could hear and understand, but she simply could not control her eyes.

We found out from the constant testing during the first couple of weeks that she was losing her sight as everything else shut down. She could not identify people as the body was just blurred. Because she was becoming blind and losing her ability to speak, the doctors assumed she was also losing her hearing. It wasn't long before she was totally paralyzed. By this time, I had even less confidence in the team of doctors. Even though I had almost zero knowledge when it came to ill health and this particular situation, it was becoming apparent that they knew little more than I did.

They sent a sample of her spinal fluid to a lab in Los Angeles. At that time, that was the only lab in the West that could do the test. We had ten long days waiting for the test results. It came back positive for multiple sclerosis, which had no known cause and no known cure.

At this point, the neurologist, who was the lead physician of the team, stood at the foot of Jill's bed and told me that there was nothing more the hospital could do and that they needed the bed for someone they could help. He said Jill would never recover and felt there was no hope she would survive. He went on to tell me that I should find an institution that could deal with the body and go on with my life.

Now that the doctor had asked us to leave, the hospital suggested I pay the bill in full. There was not even a *suggestion* as to what I was supposed to do with Jill. I was supposed to simply "find some sort of an institution for the body."

I felt really sad all the time … and empty. I did not wish to bring people around me down, so I talked to few people. In retrospect, that was a big mistake. My prayers were not being answered, and because I was very angry with God, I wasn't active about getting a prayer chain going. It was my understanding at that time that God was in total control, and if he did not cause this, he at least sanctioned it. I knew Jill to the core, and there was no way she had done anything to deserve this. I held all this in. I could not or would not accept what everyone thought was reality.

I had plenty of problems, but two were on the forefront. First, I had to find a place for Jill, and second, I found out that the insurance company had paid for nothing. Marie was very good at the details when it came to the financials. I knew every bill had been submitted with supporting documentation. She made me aware that they had paid for nothing.

I made an appointment with my insurance broker. I knew the guy pretty well as we had used our plan extensively in the past couple of years. His office was not far from the hospital on South Virginia. Actually, it was very close to Robinhood Drive, where I had met Jill.

I walked in and sat down across from him at his desk. I could tell immediately that something was wrong. "So tell me—what's going on?"

"Believe me, I have been doing everything I can. Corporate has made the decision to cancel your policy. They were worried about the open-heart surgery and where that may lead. Now it looks like you are in this for the long term. They're just not going to pay."

"I'll have to sue. They aware of that?"

"I guess they are willing to take their chances if that is what it comes to."

"All my premiums are paid, right?" He nodded. "Why are they doing this?"

"Your daughters total was six figures. This one just made six figures, and there is no end in sight. These aren't the only claims against the policy either. Please know that I have nothing to do with this decision."

"I know." I walked out, went to my car, and sat behind the wheel, my head spinning. I knew I needed to get legal action going … and soon.

I called my legal guy, the one I had used when I was going to incorporate and the same guy I used when I purchased Regional Door and Hardware. I brought him up to speed on what had happened, the diagnosis, and what had just taken place.

"You sure you paid for the policy?" he asked. I assured him my premium was paid, not only mine but all the employees I insured.

He said we could hold the hospital at bay. What we needed to do was give complete control of all assets to me as Jill's name was on everything. I would need to have her power of attorney in case I had to sell any assets. It would be a legal document if we could get a pen in her hand and help her make an X with witnesses. It had to be done prior to her passing. With multiple sclerosis, you do not get better before you die.

The last thing Jill had heard was the doctor say, "Put her body in an institution and go on with your life." Not long thereafter, I entered her room with my lawyer and witnesses and put a pen in her hand so that I could do what I needed to do, which, of course, to her meant put her in an institution and go on with my life. Because we assumed she could not hear, we did not explain what this was all about. I can only imagine the hopelessness, fear, and panic she must have felt.

By now Jill's parents were spending almost all their time trying to find a facility and/or a doctor to take Jill's case. There was no internet back then, so you simply called everyone you knew for help or information, and some of the people you talked with would call folks they knew. As Jill had with our daughter's anorexia, I went to the library to study everything I could on MS. As with anorexia, not a great deal was known about MS. The generally accepted philosophy by the medical establishment was that for some reason the immune system started attacking the patient's body. Lymphocytes in the blood that normally attacked infection were eating the myelin insulating shield from each nerve. The nerves would short out, and impulses from the brain could not control the body. Nothing I read made sense to me. Two and two did not add up to four anymore. I really felt as though something else was going on. I simply did not have any idea what. Who was I to question what these learned medical professionals were coming up with? Time would teach me to question everything.

During all this I was trying to be present with Jill, be there for Lori and Lisa, and help LaVon keep the home in some sort of order. I also had to check on the construction company, the door company, and the cabinet shop, and then I had to find time for prayer. None of this seemed to be working, especially the praying. I know they were simply trying to help, but a couple of friends suggested that maybe the doctors were right and that I should not hold on to false hope. It was almost unbelievable to me how little they understood about the meaning of true love. The chances of my ever giving up were less than zero.

Bad Talk

My stepfather, mother, and older brother were ministers. They were Pentecostal, and that was my religious upbringing. At this point, however, my religion was not working. I was told to read the book of Job. In this story God made a deal with the devil and allowed the devil to strip Job, a wealthy man, of everything, including his home, possessions, children, and servants. The object was to test Job's faith. This was the last thing I needed to hear or read. I was not willing to believe God was testing my faith, not at Jill's expense. God making a deal with the devil did not sit well with me. Some things in the Bible made perfect sense to me, and some things made no sense at all. This was one of the latter. I left the church in my mid-twenties, a bit confused about it all, and in my mind, I figured that maybe when I was forty, I would endeavor to sort it all out. At the time, that age was a long way off. Now it was a few months away. There was no time to sort now. There was too much going on in my life. Where did the last fifteen years go? It had all happened so quickly. I could never have imagined at the time that the next forty would go by even faster than the first forty had.

My religious teaching was not working. My prayers were not being answered, and I wanted them answered *now*.

I knew Jill to the core. On the inside she was the most kind and loving person I had ever met. She was the only person I knew who would go out of her way to avoid an insect on the sidewalk. All life was precious to her. With no religious teaching while growing up, she had a very real relationship with God inside her. The God I knew was an entity *up there* someplace. Jill's communication was directly to the source. Mine was through His Son, and often he seemed to do a poor job of relaying the request. I knew in my heart of hearts that I had done nothing to deserve this, and I was even surer that Jill had done less. There was absolutely no reason for this to happen from my religious point of view. I refused to believe God had made another deal with the devil.

Suffice it to say that at that time in my life, my understanding was that God was up there and that he was somehow in control of our lives. If he had not caused this, he had at least allowed it, and I was not happy about that. I remember a lot of tears and pleading with God to change what was happening. I did not like what was going on in my life.

Back when Jill was home and trying to gain strength for open-heart surgery, I had taken her to a church my mother recommended. During the prayer circle around Jill, the minister said that he saw an angel of death around her. I decided then and there that I would never allow anyone to talk "stink," as they say in Hawaii, around Jill. She was my best friend and the best kind of wife any man could dream of having. I would allow no more talk like that no matter what credentials the person had, not a medical man or a clergyman. Jill simply had to get well. I could not lose her, not now. Somewhere, somehow, I would find an answer.

CHAPTER 12

A RAY OF HOPE

Not long after I had been asked to remove Jill from the hospital and find a facility that could "deal with the body," her parents were told about a doctor in Tucson, Arizona, who had a clinic that dealt specifically in patients with MS. A friend of theirs from many years past had a cousin with a son who had been diagnosed with MS and gone to this clinic in Tucson, so they gave us the name. I called the clinic and spoke with Dr. Jerry Giordano, the doctor in charge. He said he would be happy to accept Jill at his clinic. I heard him say he would take *Jill*, not "the case." To her medical team in Reno, Jill had become "the case," not Jill. I liked the man already.

A trip of more than a thousand miles with Jill was going to be a challenge to say the least. I could not find an ambulance—air or ground—that would agree to take on the challenge. I knew the trip would be extremely expensive. At this time, I still had lots of assets, but I needed to budget my money. My banker friend had set things up so that I could borrow as needed against my assets. That being said, I needed to weigh each dollar I spent. The cost of the trip became a nonissue as I could not find an ambulance that would be willing to transport her. I think they were afraid she would expire on the way, leaving them open to a lawsuit, or maybe they found out I had no insurance. Either way, it was not an option.

As it happened, a large number of friends and the entire real estate community in Incline had offered to help in any way they could. One of these friends was a man named Jim Minesh. Jim was a realtor who had worked with Jill. He was also a retired airline pilot who owned a fairly large private airplane. I knew this plane had two rows of seats and those seats could be configured so that Jill could be prone and still leave room for a couple of passengers. For the past few years, I had been trying to find time to learn to fly an airplane. This was to have been my next venture. I knew Jim's plane was large enough, so I gave him a call.

"Jim, this is Gabe. I need to get Jill to Tucson, Arizona."

"When do you need to get her there?" he asked.

"As soon as possible, my friend. Can you fly us?"

"Can you have her at the executive terminal at the Reno airport at five in the morning tomorrow?"

"I can, and I will. Thank you."

He said, "In mid-August there are a lot of thunderstorms in Arizona, and Tucson has some of the worst. We need to get there as early in the day as possible as these storms come up in the early afternoon, and it is a five- to six-hour flight.

"How much should I budget for the trip?"

"Absolutely nothing. You get her to the airport, and I'll get her to Tucson."

Jim was one of many people who exhibited absolute kindness and generosity. When times are tough, the goodness of man can really show up in profound ways. From our earliest conversations, Jill and I had talked about the concept of "doing unto others as you would have them do unto you." I would always stop and help change a tire or make repairs for someone stranded alongside the road, even If I were in a suit and tie and running late. Now it was our turn to receive, and I was grateful.

The hospital in Reno was only too glad to get rid of *the case*. Jill was rolled on a gurney to the front door, where I picked her up and placed her in my car. This was the same way she had arrived, but she was in much worse condition now. The airport is not far from the hospital, and we were there before five o'clock. The private nurse I had hired would make the trip with us.

"Hi, Jim. This is Betty. She's a nurse and will be flying with us today."

Jim took over. "Okay, Betty, if you'll just get in the rear seat on the left side, you can support Jill's head while Gabe and I lift her to you and onto the seats that are reclined."

"This is one maneuver they didn't teach us in college," said Betty.

"I've been flying for thirty years, and this is a first for me too. We're just going to have to figure this one out as we go."

It took all three of us to get Jill in what looked like it might be a comfortable position as her body was completely limp, and even at 125 pounds, it was awkward to get her in the plane.

We lifted off the airstrip at five that morning on a completely clear mid-August day. I was so looking forward to meeting the man who had given me this ray of hope.

The farther south we flew, the darker it got. I'm sure Jim did what he could to avoid the storms; however, there is no way to describe being caught in a thunderstorm in a light plane ... or any plane for that matter. We encountered fierce winds, thunder and lightning, and sheets of driving rain so loud you could hear nothing else. There was no visual reference outside. Through it all, Jim was calm, cool, and collected.

The more the plane was thrown around, the more Jim focused on his instruments. It really felt to me as though the plane was going to come apart. If Jim had not been so calm, I think the fear factor would have been much higher. I do not know how long we flew in those conditions. Whatever time had elapsed, it was entirely too long. Finally, we broke out of the clouds, and within minutes we were right over the Tucson airport.

Watching Jim fly that airplane under those conditions was almost unbelievable and very fascinating. His training and experience were evident. The ability to do what he did was magical. One day I will learn to do that, just not today.

An ambulance met us on the runway. The EMTs extracted Jill from the airplane, placed her on a gurney, and put her in the ambulance.

I bid Jim the pilot and Betty the nurse farewell and watched as they disappeared in the north sky toward Reno. I wondered what they might encounter on the way home. I thanked God for both of them, even though my relationship with God had been strained.

The airport was on one end of town, and El Dorado Hospital was on the other. When we arrived at the hospital that had sent the ambulance, the EMTs would not unload their cargo without full payment, which was more than a thousand dollars! If this was the fee for five to ten miles, I could only imagine what the thousand-mile trip from Reno would have cost.

The Arizona desert surroundings were quite different from the California or Nevada desert. The saguaro cacti were huge and seemed to stand guard everywhere. The other unique plant life seemed to love extreme heat. The beautiful nature of this place was woven into everything, including the architecture of the homes and commercial buildings. The more I looked around, the more I could see the spirit of the people in this place. It was obvious that they cared about their surroundings, understood the natural beauty, and spent the time and money to enhance it. It felt good, and I would soon find out why.

Jill was moved on the same type of bed with wheels that had rolled her out of the hospital in Reno. The difference was that this was a very nice private hospital, much nicer than the hospital where we had just spent almost three months.

We entered the second hospital. I held my wife's hand as she was admitted and taken to an upstairs floor and to a room that would become our home for months to come. I touched her as often as I could. My hope was that she could at least feel me being there. As her body was shutting down, the doctors had determined that she was going blind. She was obviously mute, and we assumed she was deaf. Did she even know I was there?

As she was transferred to her bed from the gurney, I noticed the nursing staff was different. There seemed to be a deep level of concern for the patient. They were not rushed to get the task done and get on to the next one. When they took vitals and asked me questions about her history, they were interested in every detail. The process took a considerable amount of time. Then I thought about me. I was hungry. I had only had a light breakfast very early, and as Jim had said, it was a six-hour flight. Dr. Giordano came in. He reached out and shook my hand firmly, looked me right in the eye, and gave me a confident nod. He was about my age, athletic, and casually dressed. He moved to the side of Jill's bed and just stood there for a bit. He took her other hand and bent over, getting close. He addressed her by name, introduced himself, and said, "I know you cannot respond or even see me, but I know you can hear me. Listen carefully, Jill. I'm going to help you walk out of here. I want you to rest well until tomorrow. We have a lot of work to do. I will see you at the clinic in the morning." He spoke to her just as though she could hear fine. He looked up at me and said, "Have you had anything to eat?" I shook my head. "There is a nice cafeteria on the first floor. Why don't you get some lunch and meet me in my office in an hour?"

"Thank you. I can do that." He gave me directions and left.

I had refused to believe the test that proved she had MS. No matter what it was, I was going to find a solution or a cure. She had to get well, even if I spent the rest of my life making it happen. As long as she could breathe, I would never give up. So what this doctor had to say to Jill worked for me.

I found a very nice cafeteria, got a big plate, and sat down at a corner table again. And again, I watched people, some wait staff, some medical staff, some just waiting like me. I replayed in my mind the events since June 2, Pam's birthday, and the nightmare we had been living since. My thoughts turned to my current situation—twelve hundred miles from home and from my girls, my family, and my friends. How would my business survive if I couldn't be there at all? I felt isolated and very alone. I thought about the last ten years and what Jill had done for me as a man. She made my life complete. I knew I was in the right place.

This was the first doctor who had talked to Jill, the first one to give us any hope at all. I thought, *First, Jim, and now this doctor. Just maybe things are turning.*

I found the door marked "Dr. Giordano." He was expecting me, so I sat down to talk. First, I needed to know how he knew she could hear. I had a lot of questions.

He told me that he had started the study on MS patients because he had a friend, a fellow doctor he played tennis with, who began to lose balance, eyesight, and clarity of speech. The test results indicated MS. When the two of them found that not much was known about MS, they began to study the disease. Their research led him to build the clinic.

He also told me the philosophy of this clinic was not unlike the one that the entire medical establishment held. The immune system would turn on the body, eating the myelin shield from the nerves.

"I have read that, Doc. I understand when the myelin is gone, it's gone."

"From my experience as a doctor, if the patient has no hope, no one has hope. I prefer to think there is always hope. If I didn't think this way, there would be no reason to do what I do. I know she can hear me because she is not the first patient who had come to me unable to see or speak, and I found out later they could hear, so I simply told her what she needed to hear. I have also learned it is the patient that has to do the work. We only help.

It is generally accepted in the medical field that in a person with MS, the lymphocytes in the blood that normally attack disease and infection attack the myelin shield around the nerves instead.

I have a method of reducing the number of lymphocytes in her blood. I remove some of her blood and break it down, remove the lymphocytes, and then replace her own blood. With this process, it is our hope to impede the progression of the disease."

The last few words stuck in my brain.

He continued, "I have read the entire history on Jill's chart, including the stroke and the shunt. I have also studied the results of the lab work done on her spinal fluid, so I want to follow my protocol. Let's just say that things don't really add up. As long as we are careful with her blood, it can't hurt. That being said, I have had some people come through with some amazing results. I'm just not entirely sure why. All we can do is run my program for a while and see what happens. To a large degree, it is up to Jill. That is the best I can offer right now."

He went on to say, "You need to know that my clinic is off the hospital grounds. Even though this is a private hospital, it is an American Medical Association-approved hospital, and my clinic is not approved by the AMA or any insurance company."

I had already been to the MS Society while in Reno. That was a joke. They had no answers other than classes on how to mop the floor from a wheelchair. However, if I could see my way to a donation, maybe they could help the next poor bloke. I asked the good doctor, "Does the MS Society give you any help?" He thumbed through a Rolodex, found a number of their main office in New York, and wrote it on a slip of paper.

"It is too late today, but call them in the morning. I would like to know what they have to say about me these days. Shall we say that they have been less than supportive?

But right then, I really couldn't think about that. Jill was upstairs, paralyzed, blind, and mute. She needed someone whole in her court.

I already had a sick feeling, but I had to ask, "Okay, doc. What should I budget to run your program?"

"The fee would be separate from the hospital. Treatments will be $500 each and a patient's body could generally stand about four per week.

"What will the hospital charges look like?" I asked.

"The bed is $750 a day, but that does not include food or drugs. You can add to that any physical or other therapy. Generally, your insurance will pay a good portion of the hospital and related costs." He paused a moment. "I understand you flew here from northern Nevada in a small plane this morning. You must have rolled out of bed mighty early this morning. Why don't you try to get some rest?"

"I lie down. I even sleep, but I don't rest. I do need to find a motel. Maybe that will keep my mind occupied for a bit. I'll see you first thing in the morning."

This did not seem to be the time to tell him we had no insurance.

I did some quick calculating in my head—$7,000 to $8,000 a week, about $30,000 a month, give or take. My office overhead with wages, payments, and all was almost $40,000 a month. I would have to fly back each Friday and sign payroll and try to keep up the cash flow. I could add another $3,000 to $4,000 for hotel, car rental, plane fare, and miscellaneous expenses.

Not surprisingly, the cash flow was down. The net from the business was about half of what it needed to be to break even. Jill once had a substantial income, and that was gone. I did some additional calculating. This looked to be at least $50,000, maybe $60,000 per month, and I had no idea how long it might go on. When we left the hospital in Reno, it had already cost about $200,000. Even though we had more than a million dollars in assets, I just did not know how much my banker friend would be able to lend against all that. The whole situation was just too much to wrap my head around. I knew the insurance company would have to be held accountable at some point, but that could take years to resolve. Plus I had my reasons for not having much faith in our legal system. In the meantime, I would have to pay the bills.

I also knew I could not let the stress of it all get to me. If we were going to get through this as a family, it would be up to me. My faith in God had been shaken to the core, but I still had nowhere else to turn. I felt very alone. I knew God existed, but where was he?

The words just kept echoing in my head. *I hope to impede the progression of the disease.* Was my best hope that she was not going to get worse? This really started to settle in. No one in the medical profession had *any* hope at all, except for this guy. He had apparently seen some improvement in other patients, but he was not really sure why.

The Vision

As I walked down the hall toward the door, I tried to think of something else, anything else. I thought of the kids. Our son was on his own, working for our construction company, and he was able to support himself. However, we had three daughters in school, at home, and pretty much alone. All three were working part-time and were busy with sports. Each one was dealing in her own way with the possibility of losing their mother. All I could do was assure them I would never give up. This is not what I wanted for them, but they were going to have to assume the role of young adults sooner rather than later. All this added to the weight on my shoulders. Somehow the kids would survive, whether I was there or not. Jill wouldn't, not without me, so I was in the right place.

I left the hospital and checked into a motel. I took a shower and tried to clear my head. I just had to be with Jill. That was the only thing that worked for me. I went back to the hospital and sat and watched her breathe for a while. I went to the cafeteria and had something to eat and then returned to Jill's room until late into the night. I now knew she could hear me if I spoke to her. But I had no idea what to say. Maybe I could come up with something to say in the morning.

As I returned to the motel, feelings of despair overwhelmed me. The more those words rang in my head, the worse it got. *Impede the progression of the disease.* Those were not good words. Sleep had once been my friend. The only relief for months had been short bouts of sleep. Tonight my friend was not going to show. Despair turned to anger. Anger turned to blame. I was very angry, and God was to blame. My anger turned to rage. Blame turned to hate. This went around and around in my head until I totally lost it. I was so angry I could not cry. As much as I wanted to cry, I could not. All I could do was screech and yell into my pillow. My body would not stop contorting. I could not stand the thought that I had lost my best friend, my lover, and the mother of our children.

I had decided I would never leave Jill as long as she was alive. Stopping the progression of the disease was not good enough. My rage grew to something more. Now those uncontrollable tears came. My body was tied in a knot. I could not cry hard enough. All of the pent-up emotions and the grief I had swallowed in trying to handle all this just spewed from me. It was like the thunderstorm we'd flown through—endless pounding, sheets of tears. The anger was like Old Testament lightning, my voice the sound of thunder. I don't know how long I raged.

Then just like the storm, it suddenly stopped. All at once my body relaxed, and the tears came to an end. I lay back, and in my mind, I watched a vision of Jill and me running on the beach. The vision was real, something we had done many times in Hawaii. It was like watching both of us in a movie. I knew what we were wearing. I knew it was in the future. In some weird way, I was absolutely sure about our future together. A part of that future was us running on Kailua Beach again. Those were some of the best times of our life. That move to Kailua town on the windward side of Oahu shortly after we married was magical. And that would again be part of our future.

A peace came over me. "The peace that passes all understanding" is the way the Bible puts it. I had that peace. I slept. When I awoke, the vision was still clear. The peace was even more profound. My friend sleep had come for only a few of hours, but I was rested. I could not wait to see Jill. She needed to know. I now knew she could hear.

CHAPTER 13

A DIFFERENT APPROACH

"Sweetheart, last night I was given a vision, a most wonderful vision. We were running on Kailua Beach just like we used to. I know what you will be wearing, and it is not something you now have. This wasn't a dream or just a memory. It was a vision of our future, and it was crystal clear. It was a glimpse of our future together. You are going to smile. You are going to laugh and run on the beach. Jill, my love, you will be well again. There is absolutely no doubt in my mind whatsoever. Together we will have grandchildren and great-grandchildren. The doctor is right. You will walk out of here."

Even though Jill could not respond, I had to go with what the doctor had said the previous evening, namely that Jill could hear. If she could hear, I wanted her to know what I knew. I had just finished telling her about the vision when two of the nurses from the clinic arrived.

One of the nurses held Jill up on the edge of the bed while the other bathed her with warm, wet towels. They put her in street clothes, fixed her hair, and did her makeup. They told her she was beautiful. We all told her how loved she was. We all told her she was going to get better soon. We talked *to* her, not *about* her. They put her in a wheelchair rather than moving her on a table with wheels, the way she had been moved from test to test in months past. They had to tie her in the chair with a sheet, but it looked a lot better than being strapped to a table with wheels. We were off to the clinic to begin Jill's healing process. I knew it, and she knew it. She knew it because I was so damn sure of it. There was no question in my mind. *We would run on that beach again!*

When we got to the clinic, Jill was placed in a La-Z-Boy recliner. The staff explained to her just what was going to happen, and they assured her that his process was the key to her healing. I was able to sit with her, hold her hand, and reassure her. Everyone spoke to her as if they were sure she could hear them. Everything was already so different.

For years Jill and I had planned to be in the Caribbean to celebrate our tenth anniversary. This was to take place on October 27, less than three months away. I told her I was renewing my plans to take her there, and I felt the need to tell her again and again about our future. Now that I knew she could hear, I couldn't stop talking to her. When I thought she could not hear, I did not talk. There was still no response, but we all took the doctor at his word. Jill could hear, and if she could hear, I was going to talk to her. I loved talking with my wife, and if the conversation was one-sided for a time, that was better than no conversation at all.

I thought the needle from the machine used to draw blood was unusually large. It was hard to watch as it was inserted in her arm. The machine was switched on, and blood began to move through clear plastic tubes and then through windows in the machine. I could see the process, and I explained it all to Jill as best I could. This was a key to her recovery. Her body needed time to make more spinal fluid. The problem was not a lack of drugs in her body, and it never had been. The doctor told me he was taking her off all drugs as soon as possible. He administered pain meds as needed but nothing as strong as she had been on, nothing with a muscle relaxer. This also seemed right to me.

Even though he had said, "Impede the progression of the disease," there was something about the man that gave me the feeling he knew greater things were possible. It was something about the way he came into the room soon after Jill had been admitted and transferred to the bed, not to mention the fact that he was absolutely sure she could hear. It was the way he talked to her as though she were completely normal. He treated her with the dignity and respect she deserved, and that was something that had been so lacking.

It was now so good to see Jill dressed in street clothes, sitting in a chair. She had been lying prone in a hospital gown for months. Something about her sitting up in a recliner and dressed in regular clothes made her seem so much more normal.

I knew somehow that I needed to see her with a functional body. I needed to visualize that, and this made it much easier. If she couldn't visualize for herself, I would do it for her. Without knowing metaphysical laws, we knew visualizing what we wanted had worked. The castle was a case in point. I was very aware of how important it was to Jill after the first stroke to try to look and act normal. Being treated this way would help, and that made me feel good. For the first time in months, I felt something good was going to happen. I felt this was going to be a key to her healing. Somewhere, somehow, there was an answer, and I was dead set on finding it. Maybe this was it.

As long as there seemed to be little hope, I did not contact old friends. This turn of events made me aware that I should surround Jill with family and friends as much as I could and ask for prayer.

Jill had a very close friend in Southern California, a couple hundred miles west. Linda and Jill had gone through pregnancy together and had given birth to their babies one day apart. I called Linda and told her where we were and what was going on. She said she would be on a plane as soon as possible. I told her there was nothing she could do and that prayer would be appreciated. "I'll pray, and I will be there," she said.

The treatment on the machine that pulled her blood, separated it, took lymphocytes out, and returned her blood took a couple of hours. From the time the nurses came into her room, got her bathed and dressed, tied her in a wheelchair, wheeled her to the clinic, and set her up on the machine until the time we got Jill back to bed, half the day was used up. I could tell she was tired; so was I. So I slipped into her hospital bed and wrapped my arms around her, and we slept. This time when my friend sleep showed up, it was different. I rested.

For months, sleep had been an escape from a nightmare life. When I returned to my room, I now would dream about and look forward to running on Kailua Beach with Jill. Hell, just *sitting* on Kailua Beach with Jill would be pure heaven. Again, I rested well.

The second day in Tucson went pretty much the same as the first. The doctor was kind and caring; the staff was above and beyond. The machine that worked on Jill's blood was large and impressive. The nurse said Jill had good veins, easy to find. They all talked to her as if they were having a normal conversation with a normal person. That felt good, so very good. When we got back to Jill's room, there was a cot by her bed. The hospital advocate came in, gave me a hug, pointed to the cot, and said, "You sleep here if you wish."

"I will."

She smiled warmly and said, "I thought so." She turned and left. I stretched out on the cot for a nap.

When I awoke, Jill's friend Linda was there. We talked late into the evening. Linda and Jill had been close friends long before I met Jill, and Linda knew how close Jill and I were. If we had met in a Hawaiian setting, I would use the expression "We talk story … long time."

I gave her the key to my rental car and the key to the motel room. "I am comfortable here. I'm thinking about giving up the motel room anyway."

In the morning Linda got to the clinic at the same time we did. She let Jill know she was there and how much Jill meant to her. Assuming she could hear, she caught her up on what was happening in her life and the lives of her children. She had called the airline and found one seat back to Ontario in the midday. After a couple of hours with Jill, she called a cab and left for the airport. There was not much she could do for Jill or me, and she had children of her own to care for. At this point, she was a single mom, and the kids were with a babysitter now. The stay was short, but I really understood just how close Jill and her friend were. They were connected at a very deep level.

Sharing

On this day I would take the first of many long walks as Jill rested. The weather service reported 116 degrees as I left for the walk. I think the temperature was considerably hotter at about five feet above the pavement.

Back in Jill's room, I drank a quart of water, took a shower, and drank another quart. Then I settled down to study the hospital dinner menu for the first time. Almost anything a person could want was on that menu. Coquille St. Jacques? How perfect is this? This was a meal that Jill and I had enjoyed a number of times at an old restaurant and inn back in Verdi, Nevada. I could hardly believe it was on the menu at this hospital in Arizona. The meal was wonderful. Even the presentation wasn't all that bad.

"Jill, you are going to have to get off liquids. I do not want to eat alone any longer. I really, really want to share this meal with you."

We both knew that everything in life is better when you share it with someone you love. I was now sure that we would share life experiences once again. I just did not know when. It seemed that we had a long way to go.

CHAPTER 14

THE TEAM GOES TO WORK

This was the third day on the machine. We were almost through with the lymphocyte depletion process. As I had the first and the second day, I was holding Jill's hand, sitting as close as I could, and watching the process when I saw her move her little finger. I yelled at the doctor, "Jill moved her finger!" Dr. Girodano and the staff gathered around, and she did it again for them. There were tears, laughter, and hugs.

The staff knew exactly what to do. They immediately went into party mode. We were going to have a party. We were all going to celebrate this event so that we could remember it for the rest of our lives. If one can move a little finger, one can communicate. Jill could communicate. There were congratulations and praise. You would think she'd just finished a marathon. *And she had.*

This doctor was trained as a hematologist. How was he to know that his loving words and actions along with those of his staff had a far greater impact on the patient than any machine? That was not a part of his schooling. I was not sure what part the machine played in all this, but I knew how the people and the party made me feel. I was dead sure these people would be the first step toward that vision of my wife and me on Kailua Beach. That vision was crystal clear, not like a dream that fades. At time passed, the vision stayed just as clear.

On the fourth day on the machine, Jill gave my hand a little squeeze. We took a couple days off for rest with no clinic and no machine. Jill slept almost all day, so I decided to take another walk.

The walks would give me time to clear my mind, get away, step back, and look at the big picture. I thanked God for my ability to deal with everything that had taken place and whatever it was that was coming. I mentioned at the beginning of this story that my long walks alone in the back country were where I could connect with God better than in church or anywhere else. I was still confused about why God would let this happen. I needed to figure that out. Walking alone would give me the time not only to vent but also to listen and hear, which I did. "You both have a lot of work to do," I heard. I didn't really know at the time what that meant, but I got that message loud and clear.

I was anxious for Jill to get back on the machine for a fifth treatment. By the end of it, she could blink at will. On the sixth day, she could make a sound. It was a murmur, but it was auditable. Every day Jill was getting something back. Chewing would be good. I so wanted her to eat solid food, not just liquids.

At this point, it was obvious that she was recovering. I found the paper the doctor had given me the first day with the number of the main office of the MS Society, so I called. They said to me, "Stay away! He's a quack!" I told the doctor about my call. "I think they are afraid I may be successful here. That would interrupt the cash flow. They cannot have that. It is not the only organization that feed off people's illnesses. They talk about cures while pushing drugs that mask the symptoms at best."

There were things the body seemed to just start doing and some things that required a great deal of effort on Jill's part. Forming words was one that seemed to require great effort. The doctor ordered speech therapy since Jill had to learn all over again how to form words. Both a physical therapist and an occupational therapist were called in. These people would work on teaching Jill to sit up, hold a cup, and all the other things we normally take for granted.

I guess when the body's nerves are damaged or the brain is damaged, the body has to find a new route and remember it. It soon became apparent just how much work Jill had ahead of her. The concentration it took on her part just to move her toe or lift her hand was unbelievable. Chewing and talking were especially hard. Controlling her tongue was impossible at first. The physical therapist told Jill she would have to learn to crawl before she could learn to walk again just the way a baby learns. I have no words to describe the feelings I experienced while watching Jill fail at her first attempts at crawling.

The physical therapist was a large lady. She would position Jill on all fours in order to teach her to crawl. When Jill took the weight off one arm, she would lose her balance and roll to one side, and the therapist would then get short with her. Experiencing this when a person is six months old is one thing, but when you're thirty-two, it's quite another. I felt very bad for Jill as she would try and fail and try again to get her body to do the most basic things while working with a therapist who was frustrated and showed it. I couldn't imagine having all this take place day after day and not even be able to articulate what was going on inside.

Our three daughters all have names beginning with L—LaVon, Lisa, and Lori. At first, Jill could not form an L no matter how hard she tried. It was so hard to get her tongue to touch the top of her mouth, which was necessary to form that letter. She later told me that she was sure they'd think she'd forgotten their names since she could not say them.

The speech therapist and the occupational therapist were very patient, but we called the physical therapist "Attila the Hun." It was very hard on both of us when the physical therapist would get exasperated when Jill could not do the most basic things she had requested.

Each Friday I returned to Tahoe to look at the business, make payroll, visit with the girls, see friends, and give a report. I would pass Jill's parents in the airport on their way to Tucson for the weekend. The first time her parents could not make it, I sent the girls to Tucson. LaVon was old enough, so I left the keys to a rental car under the mat and told them where it was parked at the airport. It had been six weeks since we had left Reno with Jim in the airplane, and the girls had not seen her for a couple of weeks before that.

LaVon was almost eighteen, and Lori was thirteen when they made the trip to Tucson. Lisa, who was fifteen, was staying with her friend Tony in Las Vegas. I didn't fly her in as she did not seem to be handling the situation well. I felt she was just too emotional.

The girls had a great time pushing Jill around in her wheelchair, exploring everything they could. Jill still had to be tied in, but they had fun anyway. They were excited to see their mom out of bed, and they explored every crook and cranny in the hospital as well as the grounds around it.

When I got back on Monday, the girls and I talked about my vision. I must have sounded convincing as they decided to take Mom to the mall and buy her running shoes. It was not too far to push the chair, so we tied her in and headed for the Foot Locker.

Jill later said of this experience, "I was very aware what this shopping trip was all about. I thought that if my husband and children believe strongly enough that I will run again, this is exciting. I will do the work necessary to make it happen, no matter how hard it is. I will make it happen for me, and I will make it happen for them."

At one point, it looked as if we might not have to worry about the shoes for Jill. The girls decided at one street crossing that they could beat the light while pushing Jill's chair. It didn't look good when the light turned red, and they still had a ways to go. I stopped for a yellow, but pushing their mom, the girls bolted. All I could do was watch as things got more interesting by the moment. They made it, but not before a close call. I guess the fruit doesn't fall too far from the tree. They were as addicted to adrenaline as me!

The young man at the Foot Locker was not sure that any of us were playing with a full deck, but he did an excellent job of fitting Jill with fine running shoes.

The next stop was to buy their mother shorts. They had a great time finding just the right running shorts. They were pink just like in my vision. None of us wanted to go back to the hospital, but the shopping trip was a huge outing for Jill. She had been sleeping for more than sixteen hours a day, and the longer she was not in a prone position and still, the more pain she would endure since the brain was still resting against the skull. This was pushing the limit.

All too soon, it was time for the girls to leave. They both had part-time jobs and had to get back to their work. They didn't have much to say about the young lady I had hired to live in the maid's quarters and keep an eye on them. We talked about how things were going at home. It was difficult for them, but they assured me they could deal with it if they knew that at some point their mom would come home. I promised them I would bring her home. I was not sure about when, but I would bring her home.

I honestly do not remember much about how the girls coped with things that summer. At one point, it looked as if they had lost their mother. They were totally helpless where their mom was concerned and pretty much alone. I sometimes talk to them now about it, and bits and pieces come back; however, they don't like to think about it. As strong as I tried to look during the early stages, I'm sure they knew how I felt. They watched as their mother's body shut down, and they were old enough to understand my situation. It had to be a very hard thing for kids to experience. But seeing them with Jill and playing daredevil with the chair made me smile. Their joy was evident. They were getting their mom back.

The next few weeks were filled with long days of hard work, especially for Jill. Notably, one of the clinic's previous patients named Jan, who was just about Jill's age, came to see us. Jan was able to explain to me how it felt to live in Jill's head. She had also lost the abilities to see, speak, and move.

She was one of those who had told Dr. Girodano about her ability to hear everything during that time. She simply could not respond. She said there was no way to put into words how it feels not to know if your body is prone or not, to have no control whatsoever over any function. It had been a couple of years since she had been a patient at the clinic, but she remembered not having any idea where she was in space and time. There was no sensation that let her know what position her body was in. I had noticed that the therapist had placed a large mirror in front of Jill when she was trying to teach her to sit up. Apparently, without that reference, she didn't know what position her body was in.

Jan brought Jill some Häagen-Dazs ice cream. At the time we had never heard of the brand, but she said it had helped in her healing and recommended it. This visit was bittersweet. Jan was much better than Jill; however, after two years she still used two quad canes and found walking very difficult.

There was a good moment for me during that time. One day I was on my way up to Jill's floor when I met Dr. Giordano in the elevator. On the way up, he was very quiet. When we reached her floor, he said, "Let's stop in the lounge." We sat down across from each other, and after a moment, he said, "First, I have to tell you I have no belief in a supreme being. I think the Bible was written by man, and I do not believe in a life hereafter. That being said, I know a miracle when I see one. That is the only explanation for what is transpiring. Your wife is doing truly remarkable things. If this keeps up, I may have to rethink my belief system. By the way, you make a great team. Keep it up." I wasn't surprised by the doctor's confession. Jill had that effect on people.

As soon as enough communication was possible to ask her if she missed the intimate contact between us as much as I did, she said yes.

Our one and only date prior to marriage had resulted in the ultimate communication between a man and a woman. Relatively few people understand the difference between the fun of it and the whole process—not only desire and fun but an extension of deep communication and a way of expressing a profound and deep love for each other. There is a difference, and if you have never experienced it, you will never understand it. Jill could not walk as yet, but she let me know that she didn't need to walk in this instance and was absolutely willing to give it a try.

So I pulled the good doctor Jerry aside and asked him if any harm could come from such activity. As he and I were about the same age, he understood completely. He felt it certainly could cause no harm and that physical expressions of love could have a healing effect. He would check her out of the hospital for a night whenever I wished. That night, checking in at the motel, I asked for a room away from the office as I did not want people to see me carrying my wife into the room.

In some ways, it was like the first time. In other ways, it was nothing like any other time. This is one of the best ways of communicating one's love for another. The room had a bathtub, something Jill had not had the luxury of enjoying for many months. I drew a hot bath and placed her in the water. Everything about our little getaway gave us more resolve that we could get through this together. The night was as good as it could get, given the circumstances. It was the sweetest moment of our time in Tucson. It eventually became a part of my soul.

My emotions were mixed as I prepared for the drive back to El Dorado Hospital. What I really wanted to do was just keep driving and head north back to the Castle, home with her. However, the machine had become a big part of our life. The doctor, his staff, the hospital staff, the therapists, and the patient advocate all had become a loving family. There was a lot of work to do before we could leave, and I knew that we were getting closer every day.

Our next project was to get Jill to stand with a walker. Jill's every accomplishment made her that much more determined when it came to tackling the next task, as neither one of us had ever shied away from hard work. The amount of effort it took to do the most basic things, such as close her hand, lift a fork and direct it, get her tongue to press the top of her mouth to form an L and make a word, took incredible concentration and effort. Everything she accomplished took an unbelievable amount of work, focus, and repetition.

Jill was anxious to use the bathroom on her own. In anticipation of that event, I would hold her up on a special toilet for what seemed like forever. This went on from time to time for weeks before her body decided to cooperate. But when it finally did, she was as victorious as she was with anything else, perhaps more so. It was about recovering her dignity.

One of the hardest things for Jill was that with all that time in bed, she could not read. She had loved to read since childhood, and she never lost the desire. Our home had a large library with floor-to-ceiling bookshelves. Jill had read a great deal of what was there. She loved her library and all the books in it. The fact that she could not read made us both very sad. In the past she had always made time to read. Now all she had was time, and she couldn't read a word.

The weeks became a month ... and then two months. Now it was mid-October. Jill was already doing almost as well in two months as Jan, the lady who had come to see us, was doing after two years on her own. Jill could use a walker to get to the bathroom and actually use the toilet on her own. Both were huge successes. I informed the doctor of my plans to take Jill to St. John in the Caribbean for our tenth anniversary on the twenty-seventh. This was something we had planned for ten years, and intuitively, I knew this trip would actually help Jill heal. She needed to feel alive again. That was my first priority. Second, though, were our finances, as this stay was getting very expensive.

Later Jill said of this time, "When Gabe reminded me of our anniversary plans, I knew I would have to work extra hard to get ready. I had a much more fun goal to strive for. Interacting with others outside the hospital would not be easy, but it would be so worth it. I did not want to let Gabe down after he had done so much for me. Leaving the security of El Dorado would be scary."

Dr. Giordano was reluctant as he did not want to take her off the machine yet, but he agreed. He was now aware we had no insurance, and the medical costs related to this stay alone totaled more than $200,000. The good doctor had no idea of the company losses or the medical costs in Nevada. I kept this information close to the vest. I didn't want anything to impede Jill's progress.

The lawsuit against the insurance company had been filed. That could take years to settle, and there was no way to predict the outcome. We would work on that once Jill was well again. Although I had stayed in close touch with my banker friend who had been taking care of things from a financial perspective, I felt it best not to tell him about our Caribbean trip until we got home to Incline Village afterward. His bank had a first deed of trust on all property, which was more than $1,000,000; a lien on material in stock at the door store, which totaled $200,000; and a lien on the receivables, which were still six figures if they were good. The medical and related bills were now more than $500,000 in total, and the company losses were mounting. I knew those could be reversed once I could pay attention to the business again, but when would that be?

The Honeymoon

Leaving the hospital and the clinic was going to be difficult. Katherine, the hospital patient advocate, had become a very close friend. She won my heart the day she brought in the cot for me so I could sleep next to Jill.

After that, we talked a lot over coffee. The staff of the hospital and clinic loved working with Jill. They had never seen anyone work so hard to train the body to do the things necessary to function, and everybody's hard work was being rewarded. We had become a family. So leaving Tucson and the relationships we had developed would be difficult. We had all been in this thing together from the day we got there. No one really knew yet just how much the machine helped, but it most certainly played its part. It was scary to leave; however, we had to know if the machine was needed at this point, and I needed to stop our financial bleeding.

In the ten years we had been married, we had developed a fair number of relationships that we knew would be part of our lives forever. I had developed a deep respect for Dr. Giordano, and I was aware that he put no conditions on his love for people. Later I would understand that *love without action is dead.* This man and his clinic were love in action. In the future I would gain a deeper understanding of what I was feeling. At the time, I just knew I liked the way if felt and knew I would miss these people. In the cab on the way to the airport, we both used a lot of tissues.

With a quad cane in her right hand and me on the left to stabilize her, she could walk only a few yards at a time, but at least she could walk. The way things had been going, it was only a matter of time before Jill could start caring for herself. We would find help at home and continue the work there.

Jill and I were able to take a commercial flight back to Reno where my brother Dan picked us up and drove us to the Castle. We stayed just long enough to rest up and pack what we needed to take on a cruise. We boarded a plane in Reno bound for Florida, where we then boarded a ship headed for the Caribbean. We would celebrate our tenth anniversary there. I carried Jill up the gangplank to our room.

The ship ran into thirty-foot swells the first night out, and most everyone on the ship got seasick, including the crew and me. But thirty-foot swells have a negative effect on you only if you have equilibrium in the first place, something Jill was very short of. So even though the ship was literally being tossed up and down like a cork, it had no effect on Jill whatsoever. For once, there was an advantage to her condition!

The elevator allowed us to explore many of the ship's decks. I had to carry her on and off the shore boat and on the beach, but she was there. It was absolutely unbelievable to all who were involved, but she did it.

We had never had a real honeymoon because we were broke and in debt when we got married, and we had four kids to take care of from day one. The trip worked out to be a wonderful honeymoon for us. The experience made us realize that we had so much to be thankful for. We decided we would be thankful for what we did have and not dwell on the challenges at hand. We gave thanks for each other, our healthy children, our loving friends, the business that was still cash flowing, everything. Little did we know we were again practicing what we were to ultimately learn was simply a metaphysical law. It was the beginning of a whole new life together, one where there was no question we would be there for each other for the rest of time, no matter what happened.

It was good to be away from the hospital and good to be away from the office. It was good to be away together. The entire cruise was just perfect, an incredible vacation from it all.

Gabe, Jill, and the captain of the cruise ship—October 27, 1982

CHAPTER 15

BACK TO THE CASTLE

We were back in Incline the first week of November, just more than five months from the time Jill entered the first hospital. We were now really ready to put hospital life behind us. It was so good to be home and to have the family together again. Spirits were high, and we were all ready to do whatever it took to help Jill recover completely. None of us were *at all* ready for what happened next.

We had been home just a few days. After about day three, Jill went to slide out of bed in the morning. Her legs completely folded, and she lay helpless on the floor. I carried her to the bathroom and then back to the bed.

I had scheduled myself to go back to the office that day for the first time in months, so I called in, told Marie what had happened, and asked her to cancel all my appointments. I got back into bed with Jill, and this time we wept together. She could not even start to use the walker. I will not even try to put into words the heartbreak for everyone. There are simply no words to describe that kind of emotional pain. How can you hurt that bad for someone else?

Before we left the hospital in Tucson, Dr. Giordano and I had long talks about all possible scenarios regarding Jill's condition, and we had covered this worst-case scenario. Because Tucson was more than a thousand miles from Incline, we needed to find a hospital closer to home with a machine and a doctor willing to use it in a manner that followed the protocol. No other doctor in the country was willing to risk what the doctor in Tuscan was. The machine existed, but no one was doing a lymphocyte depletion process. Remove too many of them, and the immune system fails to work. When that happens, no one knows what's next.

However, the good doctor in Tucson had found a doctor in San Francisco who had the machine and agreed to follow the protocol. This man was working with plasma, which was a lot less risky.

The first trip to San Francisco turned out to be as interesting as our first trip to Tucson. Normally, one would simply drive from Tahoe north on Highway 267 just a short distance, catch I-80 west, and go straight into the city, an easy trip of about two hundred miles. It should take less than four hours to get to the city and then whatever time it took to get across town, depending on traffic.

First, I had to get rid of my El Camino and buy a van. The El Camino, half car and half pickup, only had two bucket seats that I could not recline, and Jill could no longer sit up. This vehicle was perfect for a contractor, but not at all good for taking a wife in a prone position for a four-hour drive. Normally, a van would not be as good as a snow vehicle. Actually, this van was much like the one I had when I met Jill, and I had driven it in the snow many times and got along with it well. Not only that but the roads in the area were usually pretty well cleared of snow.

As luck would have it, snow began falling a couple of days before we were supposed to leave for the city. It snowed heavily all day, all night, all day the next day, and all night again. It was still snowing when we left for San Francisco. January, February, and March are usually the heavy snow months in the high Sierra. This was a very early storm and a big one. The incredibly heavy snow caught the state short of plows, and there were too many accidents on I-80, so they closed the highway. I decided to take a route to the north on 89 and then down the Feather River Canyon to Highway 99 in the middle of northern California, and then go south back to I-80 at Sacramento. This would normally take about an extra three or four hours. I drove for more than twelve hours that first trip to our third hospital through blizzard conditions. We were both physically exhausted, and he were both mentally drained by the turn of events, not to mention the reason we had to make the trip in the first place.

I carried Jill into this hospital just as I had carried her into the hospital in Reno so many months earlier. My vision was still crystal clear, and this day did not fit at all—back on a gurney, back into a hospital gown, and then back in a hospital bed. It was late, and the doctor would be in the next morning. I had to leave and go find a motel or somewhere to sleep. I really needed my old friend back. Sleep is not as good if you're using it to take a break from a living nightmare, and this experience was just that.

The next morning I met the doctor. The first thing he said was, "I think this treatment is an interesting concept, but I'm not sure if it's the right approach." His program was working with the plasma, not the lymphocytes. I told him I wanted to follow the protocol Dr. Giordano in Tucson set forth. He agreed to give it a try.

He was really not comfortable with Dr. Giordano's protocol, but he had the machine and knew how to use it for our purpose. He asked us to sign a document saying we would not hold him responsible for the outcome.

This time there was a hospital gown, no street clothes and no La-Z-Boy recliner. The team was nice but clinical. Day one changed nothing. Day two was just as discouraging. Toward the end of the treatment on day three, Jill started moving things again.

Damn, the machine was part of the process. Now where do we go? What do we do? How long is this machine going to be a part of our life? Is it going to take four days a week as it did in Tucson? Do we move to the city? What do we do when the money runs out? The treatments were again $500 each plus hospital and lodging for me. What about the vision? I had been so very sure.

We stayed for the week and underwent as many treatments as Jill's body would stand, and her body responded. We had taken three- and four-day breaks in Tucson. We just didn't go anywhere.

Now we could go home for a break. When we got home, Jill was doing better. She was not as well as she had been in the Caribbean or when we had first arrived back home, but she was doing better.

When we returned from our tenth anniversary vacation, she could use the bathroom by herself. Now I was back to holding her up, as she would fall from the seat if left alone, which was not fun for anyone. Her eyesight had returned to some degree but never enough to read, not even large print. She said that the words kept moving on the page.

Opening the Mind

The problems seemed to be getting more complex every day, and there was no end in sight. We had returned to Incline the first week of November, and it was now the second week of February 1983. I do not remember how many trips we made to San Francisco during November through January and into February, but it was a lot. A good day was not so good, and a bad day was awful. Even on her best day, Jill was not in any shape to take care of even her basic needs.

By now the pain in her head had stopped, which was a positive. Her vision had returned to a large degree, but she said when she tried to read, the words would move around and look fuzzy. She could form words; however, each one would take some time, and some were hard to make out. On some days she could use the quad cane, but on other days even using the walker was difficult. She needed help to use the bathroom. That was my job, I didn't mind, but I felt sorry for her having to ask for help.

It was amazing to me that our various businesses were still functioning. I just could not give them the attention they needed. We still had a good cash flow, but it was never enough to cover everything. It had not taken very long for Jill's real estate business to grind to a halt. If I had a blueprint, I could follow it, but there was no blueprint for what was happening in our lives. We were in completely unchartered territory. I simply had nowhere to turn.

It had been about nine months of living hell when two ladies came to see us at the Castle in late February. One of the ladies was a fellow realtor Jill had worked with, and we knew her pretty well. Marcie, the other lady we had never met, worked for the Incline Village General Improvement District, which was our township government.

Jill and I sat down with them in the formal living room, which had a nice conversation area. The lady we knew, Georgia, began the conversation.

She asked, "Would you be open to hearing our stories about spiritual healing?"

I replied, "There's nothing in this world that we would be opposed to listening to at this point. We have absolutely nothing to lose."

"You're going to have to open your mind just to accept what we have to tell you."

"Believe me, we're open to anything, and I mean anything. What do you have for us?"

Georgia proceeded to tell us of a miracle healing for each of them that taken place in the Philippines. They had gone to an ashram, a spiritual healing center in the mountains just outside Baguio City.

I couldn't help it. I interrupted and said, "My understanding is an ashram is usually a Hindu spiritual retreat. Is that correct?"

She answered, "You are correct ... in part. The word came from the Eastern religion Hindu a very long time ago. In this case, it best represents what happens at this retreat. As in the Hindu religion, it is a place where spiritual teachers reside and teach about mediation and healing. In each case, it is a place located in a beautiful natural setting where people go for transformation in their lives, and in this case, it is rooted in Western religion. In every sense of the word, it is an ashram, just Christian."

"That's kind of a twist, isn't it? I have never heard the word ashram and Christian in the same sentence. Please continue."

"So here is where you are going to have to open your mind. The healers at this ashram are what this country call psychic surgeons— healers who do surgery with their hands, no tools, nothing that cuts you."

Jill was listening to every word, totally focused on Georgia.

I had been told of many *healings* that had taken placed in religious revivals and ones that my mother said she had witnessed, but nothing had ever come close to this.

"Go on. You have my interest. Tell me more about these healers and your experience."

They told us if we were to do research on these healers, all reports in the United States would be very negative. Even though there had never been a report of anyone harmed, the healers who had come to the United States were literally thrown in jail for practicing medicine without a license.

Georgia said she had been suffering from female problems, and it looked as though she might bleed to death if something were not done. The solutions that the medical community offered were not appealing.

Her friend Marcy's problem was much worse. She had been dealing with breast cancer. After a double mastectomy and a lot of chemotherapy, the doctors thought they'd gotten it all, but the cancer returned. The radiation that followed left her with no immune system and very little life force. When it returned this time, she was informed that she should get her affairs in order. Supposedly, her time was short, and nothing else could be done. The cancer was in every part of her body, and there was simply nothing left to try.

"It has been a couple of years now, and we are both healthy. I feel fine, and the doctors say Marcie is in remission."

At that point, Marcie joined in. "I'm not in remission. I am cancer-free. It won't be back. I will always be thankful for the healers at the ashram. And by the way, they work by donation only."

They gave us the names of others who had been there and had been healed. Some of these people were from our town, and some were not.

I thanked them for coming to see us and giving us the information, and I told them I would follow up. During the past nine months, I did not feel my religious teachings had been working all that well. I had spent more time in prayer during those months than I could keep track of. Looking back on it, I realize that the prayers were asking Jesus or God to change what was. I had no idea we were simply going through a huge learning experience. I didn't understand that I needed to be thankful for everything, even this experience. I should have understood the difference between religion and spirituality. Jill was by no means religious, but she was deeply spiritual. I couldn't see any reason on God's green earth how what we were going through could have any positive aspect. All I knew was I didn't like what was going on in our life, and I thought it was up to me to figure a way out.

The AMA would not support the doctor in Tucson. The MS society had only one interest—cash flow. The fundamental religious folks were all about the devil and an angel of death. We would make our own determination about these healers.

I contacted the people Georgia told us about. Everyone had made the trip because of a terminal or at least a serious long-term illness, and each one highly recommended we make the trip to the Philippines.

When I told my mother, the good minister, she informed us that she knew of these people. She said that she knew they had the power to heal, but the trade-off was that you would owe your soul to the devil for the rest of eternity. I really felt I might have made a deal with Satan himself if it would give Jill the ability to use her body again. I thought about that for a minute or two and looked at Jill for about the same amount of time. I was willing to take that chance. How could any hell be worse than what had been happening in our lives? When we got off the phone with my mother, I sat with Jill for a moment, "What do you think?"

She said, "We should go."

We had been told by one of the people we talked to about a lady from Alaska who was taking sick people as a *tour* to the ashram and the healers. Her name was Joy Mae Bowles.

I called Joy Mae on a Monday. She said she had a tour leaving San Francisco late that Friday evening. If we could be there with passports, she would take us with her group. Her fee included just a little more than the airline tickets.

Two problems came to mind. Money was tight, and the tickets were not cheap. Plus we had no passports, which usually took at least weeks if not months to procure. There was no internet in 1983, so everything was done my mail. I spoke with Jill's parents and sister. Even though they did not understand in any way, shape, or form what we wanted to do, they would give us the money necessary to get there. Then I called my banker friend. From what I knew of his connections, he might be able to help with the passports. I simply did not have the time to go through the normal channels. Once again, he said, "No problem. I can help."

The banker told me to get passport photos of Jill and myself and go to the San Francisco Federal Building on Wednesday in the late morning, and then I was supposed to call him from the lobby. I did as instructed. In minutes, an FBI agent escorted me upstairs, and I walked out with passports. I later found out why he had this relationship with the FBI. The reason is fascinating, but that will have to be part of another book.

CHAPTER 16

MAGIC IN THEIR HANDS

We were on a Philippine Airline 747 bound for Manila that Friday night. We traveled with a small group of people who were all headed to the same place for similar reasons. All were either terminally ill or suffered from a term illnesses. Almost all had an advocate with them as I was for Jill. I had lifted off the San Francisco runway many times it the past ten years. My thoughts were so completely different this time. Normally, in five hours we would land in Hawaii, deplane, take in the beauty, and know we were home. This time we were only stopping to take on fuel and then fly an additional twelve hours to Manila and then another two hours to Baguio City, which was high in the mountains. What kind of people did surgery with their bare hands? What were we getting ourselves into? We had only planned this entire trip for ten days. What would those ten days bring? I did not know that Joy Mae had made this tour more than a dozen times and that the entire excursion was planned in every detail. I thought about my long walks in Tucson and what I had been told, and I wondered how all this fit in the bigger picture.

It was about ten in the evening, and it had been an exhausting week. I watched Jill as she slept, and I thought about everything she had experienced in the nine months since her sister's birthday. Was this trip our last hope? I needed to know more about what we were going to experience.

I knew little about this lady from Alaska, Joy Mae, who had apparently made this her life's work. I couldn't wait to know more about what we were in for. As soon as we was allowed to unbuckle our seat belts, I went to her and asked if we could go to the lounge and talk. Back then a 747 had a bar and lounge in the back. As we sat down and began to talk, I felt an instant connection. I had no way of knowing that this conversation would start what would become yet another lifelong friendship for Jill and me. I couldn't believe the love and compassion I felt. I returned to my seat by my wife, feeling that peace again, the peace I had felt in Tucson. Joy Mae was one of those people who had a deep connection with God. In conversation she conveyed how God had always been very real and her connection was direct. Her time at the ashram fortified that connection. The miracles she had witnessed kept her going back. She talked of a deep respect and love for the healers. She gave me confidence that we were in the right place and doing the right thing.

The 747 needed to make a stop in Hawaii going both directions. I had called Mac and Marilyn, our friends and neighbors from next door when we lived in Kailua town on Oahu, to set up a place to stay on the way back. As a senior employee with United, Mac was able to access any part of the airport for any airline. During our stop for fuel, he surprised us. He drove to the Honolulu airport and came on board for a surprise visit with us during the layover. Only a good friend gets up at 2:30 in the morning and drives across an island to spend an hour and a half with you. We were both deeply touched.

We flew on to Manila, where we were had to stay over for a day, and then we took a smaller plane to Baguio City. Joy Mae had everything set up. A bus picked us up at the airport in Baguio and took us to the ashram. The reception there was in many ways like the one in Tucson. The love and acceptance were unmistakable. So far, everything was going well. We gathered in one large room where we were given a general description of where things were and an itinerary for the next ten days. We would learn about the healers and what we could expect from them later in the day.

From there, we were shown our rooms for a much-needed nap until an informational gathering late in the afternoon. Our room was small, and it had its own bath. The accommodations were humble but clean. Everything was very simple. We had an idea about what we were in for, but we needed to hear it from the healers themselves. Everyone had told us that they only accepted donations, and of course, we were concerned that they'd request a hefty donation.

What happened in the next ten days will likely give some people reason to question if any of this story is true. As God is my witness, I've described what happened in the next ten days exactly as I remember them. I had been a bit of a camera buff since I could afford good equipment. The camera I carried was one used by many professionals. I had with me an assortment of lenses, 28 mm wide angle, 35 to 200 mm telephoto, and I could double that to 400 mm. If I was allowed, I would document this trip. Not only did they allow me to document everything, but they also encouraged it. We have an entire photo album devoted to this trip. (VHS motion had just been introduced, and I had one of those cameras too. I didn't take that as it took up a suitcase of its own at the time.)

Late that first afternoon in the ashram, we were all gathered in a room that would double as a classroom and a dining room, and then we were given our first real insight into what we were in for. We found ourselves in a room with people who had traveled from every corner of the earth—Down Under, Japan, England, Sweden, among other places, and of course, the United States. In each case, this was their last hope.

First, we were introduced to the man who was to be our spiritual teacher for the next ten days. This man had been the right-hand man to Ferdinand Marcos, president of the Philippines. He had been the equivalent of a five-star general and the head of the military schools, and he had also written the speeches Marcos delivered. His name was Sante (pronounced San tee).

When the US military entered the Philippines during the Second World War and removed the Japanese, who had moved in and taken the country from the Spanish, they found the leaders of the Philippine guerrillas and put them in power to run the country. Marcos and Sante were among those. Sante had been an extremely powerful, angry, and evil man. As a lad, he had seen the atrocities inflicted on the Philippine people by the Spaniards. The Japanese invaded, and they defeated the Spaniards. They treated the local people even worse. They provided no education, no rights, and no medical services. They used the women, and any man who protested was dropped in a cistern, which was a concrete structure about ten square feet positioned on the seashore at low tide. The Japanese would drop men in from the top and close the lid. When the tide came in, they would drown. Someone would open a door on the side afterward, and the bodies would wash out to sea. He watched this and decided it was his job to take revenge. The US military had handed him a position of power, and he used it.

He had a wife and daughter he loved very much. They decided they could no longer deal with his anger, so they left him and joined a religious group as Christians. In an effort to get his family back, he started spending time with their newfound friends. I wish I could relate the story as he did at that time. Suffice it to say that he inspired the name of this book. When we met him, he had already started his mission to become as much like Christ as possible, a quest to right every wrong he had ever done, and he had done some really bad things.

We learned then that the pendulum always swings in both directions. The farther it goes in one direction, the farther it swings in the other. This man was an exceedingly kind soul. He was not only highly educated but also very wise. His understanding of how the physical and spiritual worlds were interconnected was indeed clear. It would be necessary for us to have our own clear understanding of this to comprehend what the healers did. It did not take long to develop a deep respect for the man.

His first talk immediately put me at ease. He started it all by opening a Bible to the book of John and quoting the words of Jesus, a passage taken from a part of the Bible I knew well. "Even the least among you can do these things that I do, and even greater things." Jesus was teaching by the Sea of Galilei after healing several people, including a blind man.

He said, "It is all about as simple as that. The healers are simply taking the words of Jesus and putting them into practice. You have to know that nothing in this world is solid, not even you. It takes healers two or three hours of meditation to raise the frequency of their bodies prior to removing from your body things that are keeping you from being healthy.

"There will be blood but no pain, no scare. Each person who is here for healing will experience two surgeries each day for the next ten days. They use no instruments, only their hands. Each will be preceded by a time of prayer prior to entering the healing center and again at the center." He went on to say there were some things we would need to know to keep from getting sick in the future. There would be afternoon classes on that. Next he told us how the healers came to be.

When the Spanish conquistadors conquered the Philippines in the 1500s, the native people were given no rights. Anyone who resisted was brutally victimized. The women were used, and none of the natives were given an education or medical treatment. During the four centuries that followed and prior to the Japanese occupation—in which they were treated even worse—the Philippine healers emerged. One healer could see many people per day. These people would leave well, and with the proper education, they would stay well.

In the next ten days, we would learn new things about love. The first step was to learn to love yourself as you were. If you wished to be well, you needed to start there. Jesus taught that you should "love others as you love yourself." I think somewhere along the line, we have lost what it means to love ourselves. You must love yourself in the body you have. He said you should love others without any conditions. You cannot love others unconditionally if you do not love yourself first.

Sante also said, "Love without action is dead, and your understanding of all this will be a key in the healing process. It means doing what is necessary to keep your body and your mind in the best possible shape for the years it has on it."

I immediately thought of Dr. Giordano, his love in action, and the results. I mentioned he had the body of an athlete. By action, I mean that he took care of himself and did what he knew worked in taking care of others. He was active in all that. By the end of the first class, I was absolutely sure the devil had no part of this. By the end of the stay, I was certain that the devil had no power that I did not give him. By the end of the class I felt sure Jill would be healed. No wonder Marci made the statement. "No remission. The cancer is gone." She knew it. She had been here.

The first operation included work on her temple areas and the third eye. They also worked specifically on Jill's left eye for the removal of blood clots. After the procedure, they placed a large gauze patch over her entire eye. Even with the eye patch, she felt more stable. Prior to that, even standing in one place, she did not feel stable. She always needed someone or something to hold on to. When they removed the patch the next day, they handed her a book. If she covered her right eye, the words no longer moved around he page. Jill could finally read again, even if only from the left eye. It was not yet perfect, but there was a huge improvement. The changes were profound. Reading and standing erect by herself without the feeling that she may fall—these were enough that we were anxious to experience what was coming next.

After the first psychic surgery, Jill wore a patch on her left eye.

In ten days, there were twenty visits to the healing room. Each time the healers used bare hands to remove blood clots and some tissues from critical areas of the body. Each day Jill could control her body a little better. Bending over and shuffling like an old person was being replaced with a more fluid stride. She had not used her muscles since June of last year. They need to be exercised. She had no stamina. However, each day it took me just a little less effort to help her with her walking. I always stayed very close, and I was encouraged to take pictures of whatever I wished. We were very comfortable with what we were experiencing.

About midway through the process, the healers suggested I get on the table. I was not afraid. I simply did not see a reason. "Please," they said. "You are here, so you may as well get a tune-up." So I got on the table.

After scanning my body once with the hands close to my skin, the healer went for my left shoulder. I had been living with that problem with the shoulder from the time I had fallen while waterskiing in the middle of Lake Tahoe. The second injury on the ski hill happened not too long before we left for the Philippines.

Even though I had not mentioned it, the healer took mere moments to focus on the shoulder. As Sante had said, there was some blood, no pain. I did feel a sensation not unlike that of a deep tissue massage. It felt as though they were pressing hard, but it did not hurt. Immediately, when the area was cleaned of blood and tissue, it appeared as if nothing had happened to the skin. Not long thereafter, I had full range of motion. My strength has since returned, and to this day, I have never again had a problem with my shoulder. It was the only thing they found to work on. It took more time in prayer than it did to do the surgery.

Almost everyone at the ashram played their part in the process. The tiny lady, who had been in Baguio since long before the Second World War, came to each room, and for twenty-five cents, she gave you a massage. The boys who played music for us in the evening and during the day made sure we had everything we needed. I could always hand one my camera if I wished to be in the image. Both young men and young women helped. These kids, Joy Mae, the teachers, and the healers all played their parts. We learned many lessons in the ten days we were there, not the least of which was about love and the healing power of love. We also had lessons about nutrition and how we didn't need to consume red meat for the body's nutrition. We learned about maintaining a diet of fruit and vegetables, nuts, grains, and green things. Sante talked about keeping one's life in balance, getting the proper rest, exercising, and meditating to keep the body functioning. He talked about the importance of positive thoughts and how everything started with a thought. He had so much wisdom to convey.

Unconditional love of the self, others, and all things—this was the key to any healing and ongoing wellness. And remember, love without action is dead. It became apparent that the love we experienced in Tucson had a great deal to do with the healing that happened there. Love leaves no room for guilt, resentment, fear, anger, or self-pity. Forgiveness is huge, and it is a must if you hope to be well. Long-term resentment can cause illness, even cancer.

As things at the ashram progressed, I felt really good about Jill, the strides she was making, and her future. Even though I thought I held it all in pretty well, I constantly thought about the huge debt we would face when we returned home. While having lunch with Sante, he casually said, "Something is bothering you, something not related to your wife's healing. Am I right?"

"I am going to face a very large debt when I return—part of it medical, part of it business-related. I am trying to figure out how I am going to deal with it. It is bothering me a lot."

"Here is what I think you should do. Don't try and figure it out. Determine the outcome you wish to see, tell God, and get out of the way. Turn it over completely. Thank him for where you are in all things, and let him work out the how. Learn to live in a place of gratitude. Let go, and let God."

"I'm awfully close to this, and there are quite a few families counting on me. I hear what you're saying. I will do my best."

Our last day at the ashram in the Philippines

Our experience in the Philippines is difficult to put into words. To say it was life-altering would be an understatement. Nothing about our life has been the same since. We find it interesting that some of our friends and acquaintances have remained just that but wish to avoid discussion of the trip to Baguio City. Others have avoided us because they think there is something just too spooky about our experience. There are relatives who believe we made up the whole thing. These same relatives obviously have no concept of unconditional love. They hold in hate and judgment toward other family members for decades on end. Those who choose to think this way have illness in their own lives and will not discuss forgiveness or removing the conditions attached to what they think is love. There are far too many people in this world who do not love themselves and therefore cannot love others. Then there are those who love to hear the story, want to discuss it, and wish they could have been part of it.

Spiritual healing methods, such as psychic surgery, are illegal in the United States. The American Medical Association has a tremendous amount of pull with lawmakers and has seen to it that the competition is eliminated. Healers who come to the United States are most certainly going to be jailed if they are caught. Isn't it interesting that no person has been harmed by one of these spiritual healers while thousands and thousands die needlessly in hospitals every day because of negligence, mistakes, and a host of other unnecessary reasons? The hospitals are legal, and the healing rooms are not. As long as industries can buy lawmakers, this state of affairs will remain the same.

This experience made me want to study the subject. I will share just one example—and there are many—of how the bankers have hijacked our medical and education systems.

In the 1950s, Dr. Max Gerson found a cure for cancer. He found that by cleansing the body and loading it up certain nutrients, most cancer would go away. The only people who were difficult to cure were those who had undergone *conventional* Western treatment. Representatives from our government tried to stop him from practicing medicine, but he continued using only prayer, diet, and visualization. He resisted the demands put on him by the AMA and the government. He passed away at a young age under the most unusual circumstances. His daughter moved the clinic to Mexico and has continued his protocol to this day. I have intimate knowledge of this clinic because my sister-in-law went there to study and learn how to do what they do. If you wish to become a practitioner, you are required to go through the program at the clinic just as if you were a patient. Nothing about the process will do anything but bolster your immune system. The Gerson Clinic has not only a lot to do with the spiritual aspect but also everything to do with cleansing and nutrition. Not one soul has ever been harmed, and too many to count have been healed. Yet it is still illegal in the United States. As with the Philippine healers, not everyone is healed. It would seem that some people have a previous agreement. At least that is my take.

There are many clinics just outside the US border with different modalities and programs with notable success rates when healing long-term or terminal illnesses.

We have lost touch with the Philippine healers. Our tour guide, Joy Mae, still lives in a remote area of Alaska. She is in her ninth decade now, and we still stay in touch. We can never thank her enough for getting us to the ashram and the healers there. She served as an angel to many people.

This would be the start of an entirely new life, the start of a whole new learning experience.

On our way home to Tahoe, we stopped in Hawaii to spend a few days with our close friends Mac and Marilyn and of course, our friend and business partner Roy. I know our story was very strange to Marilyn, who was a nurse, but she supported us completely, which was clearly an example of unconditional love. She was like a sister to Jill, and she still is. We have spent many days at their home, and their family has stayed many times at the Castle. We have found the rare but great value in friends who will remain just that, no matter what you are going through. When you find friends like these, you cherish them.

During our stopover in Hawaii, Jill was able to walk from where we were staying to the beach. She needed an arm to hold on to, but she could walk under her own power. It was about two long city blocks, and she made the walk with some help, especially when it came to walking in the sand. She was able to sit, talk, and read. Just observing that gave me great pleasure. It was, however, necessary to get the car to bring her home as she was too tired to walk. She still had little stamina as she had spent the better part of nine months in bed or just sitting.

Before the trip to Baguio, she slept for at least sixteen hours a day. Now a typical eight hours would rest the body, but she would run out of energy pretty fast.

She had vastly improved, but she still needed time to work on her fine motor skills and to build up the strength in the muscles needed for balance. She was doing better every day, and based on what had happened at the ashram, we felt sure that a completely normal and functioning body was not far off. Through it all she looked beautiful; it was just that her beautiful body failed to function.

We left a car at my parents' home in Pioneer during our trip to the Philippines. When we returned, we landed in San Francisco and transferred to a commuter plane to Sacramento, where my brother Dan picked us up and drove us to our parents' home. After a short visit with them, skirting the conversation about the whole "devil" thing, we set course for home—Incline Village and the Castle.

As luck would have it, less than an hour's drive up Highway 88 and right on the way is Silver Lake, where we shared our first and only date and where it all started. We were driving from the west, and as the lake came into view, we saw that the shadows were long on Thunder Mountain just east of us. It was much earlier in the day as this was March. We sat in the car at the water's edge as there was a lot of snow on the ground. The lava cliffs on the west side of Thunder were very black against the snow, which had fallen on both the frozen lake and the mountains. The blue sky was a sharp contrast. We sat and talked for a while about our time together since we had enjoyed our first and only date in the same spot just more than ten years earlier.

"If you knew then what you know now, would you make the same decision?" she asked.

"Absolutely. I told you that day I would take care of you and your children as long as I live, and I meant it. That *commitment* is really important to me. I trust you now understand how important."

"I do. When I first listened to you tell about how your father left his family when you were not yet six, leaving your mother to raise five children by herself, and your vow to see things through when you made a commitment, I had no idea how that would play out in my life. I think I can thank your father for being who he was. Had he not been, you may have opted for the easy way and taken that doctor at his word and found an institution for my body."

I wrapped her in my arms. "The thought never occurred to me. I have a gut feeling we are going to be together for a very long time. We have not as yet run on Kailua Beach, and my vision is still clear, so that is in our future. Based on the past two weeks, I believe illness is in our past. I'm really looking forward to a whole new life together. I think our next issue to tackle will be finances. At this moment in time, I'm not just sure what our financial future holds. Right now it's looking a bit grim."

She gave me that look, the one that said, "Are you ever going to get it?" She said, "I am so looking forward to that challenge. I love the way God has shown up in our lives. I suggest we simply focus on what it is we wish to see happen, watch for the opportunities, and go for them when they show up."

I held her at arm's length. "I wasn't going to mention it, but the unpaid bills at home are somewhere around a million dollars, maybe more. You had enough to deal with without having to think about that too."

"Tell you what I'm going to do. I'm going to work on my body, get it to where it once was, and turn the financial problems over to God. You know what I want to do right now?"

"What would that be, Jill?"

"Go home and see my kids, have a normal dinner at home, and crawl into my own bed with my husband. It feels like a whole new life in front of us."

Some Concerns Remain

The one thing that still concerned me was the hole in Jill's heart. The first stroke—the one that I was sure really happened—had done major damage to her brain. We needed to know that she would never have another stroke. We didn't even want to think about entering a hospital for open-heart surgery.

A couple years later, while we were in Phoenix, a sixteen-year-old girl who was on her maiden voyage by herself with her mother's car ran a red light and hit Jill's car between the front and back door on the driver's side. The seat belt undoubtedly saved Jill's life, but it left pain in her chest. The doctor at the emergency room sent her to the Mayo Clinic, which was not far away, as he could not find any reason for the pain. Staff members at the Mayo Clinic ran every test they could to find a cause, and they only found that her chest was bruised from the seat belt. They also could find no indication that there had ever been any problem with her heart.

We noticed other changes as a result of the time we had spent with the healers. Her breasts had always had lumps of fatty tissue that gave us cause for concern, but those lumps were now gone. For the first time in her life, her cycle became a regular twenty-eight-day event without the cramps and pain that had always been a part of that process.

By mid-1983, Jill was a different person than she had been in early 1982. She told me that toward the end of the second hospital stay in Reno, her focus remained on taking the next breath. She knew that all she had to do was give up that focus if she wanted to spend the rest of eternity with her beloved grandmother, with whom she talked while she was there. Her grandmother told her that her work on earth was not yet finished.

Jill made a conscious choice to come back and finish what we had started together. We were here to learn, and we were here to teach love and natural health education. Before we could do that, we had other things to learn. For Jill, real estate would be in the past, and natural health education would become part of the future.

CHAPTER 17

THINGS TURN AROUND

It was late March 1983, ten months since Jill entered the hospital in Reno for the first time. It felt really good to be home, the family living with real hope for the future, united once again. LaVon was nineteen and wanting to start college, but as things were, money was in short supply. So at this point, she would have to work her way through school. Because her mom had been so ill, she had to take on the role of an adult, run the household, and help her younger sisters with the problems teenagers encountered. These were things a mother usually did, but LaVon seemed to cope with it extremely well. I don't remember why, but she wanted to go to school in San Diego. So she made plans to head in that direction.

I had two major problems. The one thing the healers and the doctors agreed about was that Jill needed to get more oxygen to her brain. Our Tahoe home was at almost seven thousand feet in elevation. This was a huge problem since most of our business was there and moving the business would be a challenge. We could move back to Reno at 4,500 feet in elevation and work at Regional Door. However, neither of us liked Reno, and oxygen at that elevation was still half of what we could get at sea level. Regional Door was not going to pay off an extra million-dollar debt plus its own balance any time soon. The big problem was our short-term debt. I had a rough idea what it was, but I needed to talk with the banker and find out the exact total. The outcome of the lawsuit with the insurance company was still a big unknown. There was no reason in the world for them to cancel the policy, but it could take years to resolve that. They obviously had the best lawyers money could buy to defend their position. Cash flow was down, as I had not been able to hustle new work.

I called the bank president and told him we were back from the Philippines and what had taken place and told him that Jill was getting better every day. It was time to talk about where to go from here. I also told him of the healer's suggestion that we get Jill to a lower elevation, preferably close to sea level.

He gave me an appointment at his office in the Bay Area. When I got there, the meeting included a department head from every department in the bank, and this was not a small institution. He wanted me to meet each one. I met the department head of the real estate division, the head of the business loan department, the head of the credit card department, and a personal banker assigned to me and others. As each officer presented his department's statement of my account, the CEO stacked it with the others. They were all assured we were there to work out a repayment plan. He wanted me to meet each one as we would be working together during a "workout agreement," as they called it. This agreement would be between me and the bank. It would spell out how and when the debt would be retired. When the last statement of my accounts was presented, the department heads were excused. The only ones left in the office were the president and me.

He totaled everything up—everything the officers brought and the unpaid bills he asked me to bring. (Marie had handed them to me as I left for the meeting.) It totaled just a bit more than $1.1 million. With a huge knot in my gut, I asked as calmly as I could, "What do you think?"

Without missing a beat, he said, "You need a construction project that amounts to at least $10 million or more with a solid 15 percent for overhead and profit. If it's run properly, you can run the project out on 5 percent for overhead, and the 10 percent profit will retire this debt and do it in a reasonable amount of time. The profits from sales of the homes will be an added bonus, and they should be substantial. I have builders who turn those numbers consistently, and we all make money on the deals." He looked me straight in the eye and said, "I don't see a problem here, do you?"

"Ah, if you don't see this as a problem, neither do I."

He leaned back in his huge chair and said, "Your first job is to find a project as close to sea level as you can. And when you find one that makes sense, I'll fund it, and you'll build it." He turned and looked out the window. His posture told me what he just said was no big deal to him.

I had learned he had complete control of this savings and loan institution. I knew it had billions in assets and many branches serving many clients. Some of those clients were big builders, so it looked as though I was going to be one of those.

He swung back around to me. "The future is very bright for both of us. So go find a project, and let's go to work." He stood and held out his hand. When I shook his hand on the deal, I got the same feeling as I had with Hudson, and it felt good.

On my way home to Tahoe, I didn't know whether to cry, laugh, scream, or try to act like what had just taken place was somewhere close to normal. I had just been commissioned to go buy at least a $10 million construction project, and Jill and I would be the owners. I thought about the team of players I had to work with and realized I had almost everyone necessary to pull this off.

As I thought of Jill and the incredible progress she was making, not to mention the fact that our financial future was absolutely taken care of, the same peace came over me that I had felt after the vision in Tucson. Sante, our teacher in the Philippines, had convinced me that God wanted for me what I wanted for myself. He said it was up to me to keep the faith. This was the same thing my banker friend had said when the whole thing started. My job was to get clear on what it was I wanted, not to worry about how it was going to happen, and to take the opportunity when it presented itself. There was no question in my mind that I was going to take this one. I could hardly wait to get back to the Castle and see Jill. She would be very anxious to hear about the meeting with the bank.

When I entered the house, I found Jill in the kitchen, picked her up, and carried her to the den. I sat down with her on my lap and squeezed as hard as I thought she could stand. When she finally pulled back, she brushed a tear from each of my eyes and said, "Is it really good or really bad?"

"Sweetheart, it's both. I have never had such mixed emotions in my life. You know how much I love Tahoe and the lifestyle we have."

"Go on," she said. "Go on."

"Well, we're going to have to move. I don't know for how long. That part makes me sad. But here's the good part. Remember the deal we had with Hudson for half the construction profit on just more than $3 million in construction?"

"Yes, I do, and that was a good deal. So what does that have to do with your meeting?"

"Well, we've just been commissioned to purchase a construction project more than three times that size, and we don't share the builder profit with anyone. It will be our project, both construction and sales this time. The profit from the construction alone is more than enough to retire our debt. The net profit from sales of the homes we build should be somewhere between one and two million. I have run the numbers, and if they are correct, it could be more. Is that too good to be true or what?"

She said it again with a big smile, "You are never going to get it, are you?"

"I'm trying, honey. I'm trying. But this one is outrageous. I mean over-the-top outrageous." The hug she then gave me was proof positive that her strength was returning.

Being home was good, and my heart was warmed even more so when we were told that prior to our trip to Baguio while we were spending so much time in San Francisco for Jill's treatments on the machine, the realtors in town had created a schedule so that teams consisting of one guy and one gal would volunteer to take Jill to the city for treatment and stay as long as necessary. The schedule covered the next year. There were about a hundred people licensed to sell real estate in that town. Not everyone was active, but most were on that schedule. I couldn't even respond. Tears had come all too often in the past few years, some of sadness, some of joy, and some tears of gratitude. This was one of those times. These were the kind of folks who lived in the small town of Incline Village in the early 1980s. In a small town like that, people simply pitched in and helped others whenever they saw the need.

I hired a friend I knew had a talent for finding the right project, gave him a car and money for expenses, and sent him to the central valley and the coast of California. His job was to find a project for at least $10 million in construction cost with good profit potential and one that was preferably ready for building. I went about the business of cleaning up all the work that was in progress at home. The door company had not been covering its expenses, and it was going to require serious restructuring to get in the black. The business could have been a good one if it had had no debt and if we had been dealing in a decent economy. But the profit margin was just too thin to service the debt. I hired a new manager and told him that if he could turn a profit, he had a job. If not, we would shut it down.

Most of the contractors in the country had gone broke during the past few years as a result of government actions, and I had a few other problems to deal with on top of the bad economic situation. Because the economy had been so bad in recent years, there were a number of good projects that banks had foreclosed on and could be purchased for pennies on the dollar. My bird dog guy, the one I sent in search of a project, ran into a fellow named Norm Matson, who had his finger on the pulse when it came to the kind of projects we were looking for. So it didn't take long to identify one that would be perfect for our needs. Mr. Matson was to become a big part of our life in the decades to come. He owned a factory that manufactured components used to build dwelling spaces that were superior in every way to normal construction methods.

The project he referred us to was a 250-unit condo community with most of the first phase of seventy-five units completed. Not all the completed units were sold. The property had been foreclosed on, and it was in the hands of a judge. It was the job of the judge to sell it for at least enough to retire the debt against the property—or more if he could get it. The debt was just more than $1 million, much of which was superfluous bank charges. As it stood, the project was worth at least $2.5 million. Someone had lost a great deal of equity. The completed units that were unsold were worth almost $1 million by themselves. The property for the remaining units was worth at least $1.5 million at minimum in the current market. The market was showing signs of recovering, so if we could purchase it for anywhere close to what the bank required, the deal would be a steal. I ran the numbers, and it turned out construction costs would be about $12 million. The market would stand a 30 percent gross profit margin or about $15 to $16 million total in sales. Net profit to us after all loan charges, sales, and other costs would be in the neighborhood of $2 million. It was exactly the kind of deal the president of the bank wanted. The property would be auctioned off in court very soon.

When the day came, the bank president sent his real estate chief with me to try to make the deal. The judge started out the bidding at $1 million, and I bid that amount.

The judge said "I have a million. Do I hear a million two hundred thousand?"

Some guy said, "A million two."

"I have a million two. Do I hear a million five?"

I looked at the banker, and he nodded. I said, "A million five hundred thousand."

The judge said, "I have a million five. Do I hear a million eight?"

The other guy said, "One million eight hundred thousand, Your Honor."

At this point, I was starting to feel as though we may have made a bad choice. At $2.5 million, this would not be a good deal anymore. Where do I stop? At $2 million? I needed time to think.

The judge stopped the process, looked at the other guy, and said, "Do you have a million eight hundred thousand dollars?"

The man said, "I have a million two and six hundred thousand in diamonds, Your Honor."

The judge looked at me and asked, "Do you have a million five hundred thousand dollars?"

The real estate chief stood and said, "I am his banker, and we can tender a draft today, Your Honor."

"Sold at one million five hundred thousand." The judge struck his gavel once and then left.

I thought to myself, *I have some work to do, but it is possible we may have just made about $1 million up front on this deal. This is going to be fun. God, things can turn around fast. Or maybe a better way to put it is this: God can turn things around fast.*

The project was in Central California, specifically in Salinas, located just minutes east of Carmel-by-the-Sea. The thought of living in Carmel for a time sounded okay to me. Carmel and the Monterey area were both beautiful. Jill loved the whole area, but she set her sights on Carmel. As far as she was concerned, that was where she wanted to be. We had been to Carmel and studied the architecture of the homes prior to building the Castle. We both loved the feel of the town, so I was in complete agreement.

There was nothing to rent in Carmel, and there were very few homes for sale. All homes in Carmel were very expensive, and the closer to the ocean, the higher the price. Jill soon found the perfect house. It was very close to the beach and was a lot of money for a small Tudor cottage. We decided would try to rent that house, as it was not yet time to buy. So we contacted the owner and told him we wished to rent his home. He said he was not going to be in Carmel for quite some time and had not imagined finding a renter who would take it long term and could afford to cover all his costs.

I explained that we had just signed a construction contract for $12 million on what was potentially a project worth $16 million. I told him that we were the owners and the contractor on the project and that we might talk about buying his house later. He really didn't wish to sell the house and agreed to rent it to us. It was exactly what Jill had envisioned and prayed for.

We had learned that when people set their minds to an outcome and truly believed something particular was what they want, they could achieve their goal. Enough emotion could speed up the process. Jill had decided she really wanted that house, and she got it.

I left a foreman to finish up in Incline, hired a new manager for the door company, sold the cabinet shop, hired a housekeeper for the Castle, and moved my family to Carmel. We left the house furnished as I did not wish to sell it ... ever. When we got the debt resolved and Jill was 100 percent well, we would return. At least that was the plan.

It was really good to get back to work full-time and be able to really focus on what I was doing. This was going to be a high-production, cookie-cutter project, which was what I had a lot of experience with. Getting back into the swing of things took no time at all. We set up an office in one of the completed units in the project and brought Marie in as the bookkeeper. We needed to hire a person for the front office to work as a personal assistant and handle communication with employees, subcontractors, and suppliers and all the paperwork associated with them and their orders.

Remember the guy who sold us the blue boat because he was moving to Carmel? Well, his wife—one of those on the beach and the houseboat at Oroville—used to work the front desk at the county building department, which took care of building permits for Washoe County and Incline. If I ever needed anything done quickly and correctly, she was the lady to get it done. She was the best front office person I had ever known, and now she lived in Carmel. I was able to employ her as the office manager, and I also hired an older contractor I knew from Reno as a superintendent. He knew all the good subcontractors and suppliers.

If you wish to get things done in a hurry, you pay well and on time. As a result, the project got off the ground very fast. We started with the first phase of seventy-five units and fast-tracked the buildings that would house the models. We had those completed and furnished in four months, and then we hosted a grand opening in June.

One of the things Jill liked was decorating, and she was good at it. She didn't do all the models, but the ones she did complete were the ones that received rave reviews at our grand opening. This was a perfect job for Jill as all she had to do was pick colors, fabrics, and furniture. She would go to the store, pick things out, and have them placed in the condos. Jill was beginning to fill all the roles she had played in the past. The kids had their mom back, and I had my friend, my business partner, my wife, and my lover.

Jill decided not to go back into real estate. As a result of what we had been through in the past year, her interest had taken a whole new direction. Jill was going to study everything she could about natural health, including diet, exercise, meditation, and natural medicine. Because of what Santee had introduced us to with regard to metaphysical laws, she had taken a keen interest in that study. She now understood the importance of touch and wanted to learn therapeutic massage.

Everything was falling into place with the business, and Jill just kept improving. As in the beginning of her recovery back in Tucson, some things came easier than others. It was just as hard for her to learn—or relearn—skills as it is for a four-year-old. If you fall when you are four, it's not a big deal, but when if you fall when you're thirty-three, it is. When I met her, I found that she was one of the best female drivers I had come across. That skill was just gone now. She had to learn it all over. She tackled each task and worked at it with dogged determination until she mastered it. Driving again was very important as she made the decision to attend

Twin Lakes College of the Healing Arts in Santa Cruz, which was just less than an hour north up Highway 1 along the coast. She would get certified in hypnotherapy and massage therapy, learn hands-on healing, and graduate with a degree as a natural health educator. She accomplished all that, and she's now in a never-ending study of all her newfound interests. It is astonishing just how little is generally known about nutrition in Western culture. A doctor can go to school for eight years and get only eight hours on the subject, and yet it's vitality important to both healing and health. All the aforementioned had to do with getting healthy and staying that way. I definitely reaped the benefits of good nutrition.

Before we left Incline Village, someone told us to look up Alan Young, a spiritual healer who lived in Carmel. The day we went to sign up for a mailbox at the post office, we saw a flyer for a three-day workshop on spiritual healing at Allan's home. His home was on the same street as ours. This profound workshop was based on his book *Spiritual Healing*. He was our first real teacher at home in the study of metaphysics. During the next weekend, James Alpert, the leader of the Arizona Metaphysical Society, was giving a workshop in Carmel, and we went. He really piqued our interest as he cited so many stories of how practical application of the laws made such a difference in people's lives.

I read Dan Millman's book *Way of the Peaceful Warrior*. I loved everything about that book. The next weekend he was in Carmel at the library for a book signing. We went to that, and shortly thereafter, we attended a three-day intensive workshop in Monterey with him.

We attended the local Church of Religious Science in Monterey. Rev. Bill Little was the minister. On Monday through Friday, he taught advanced calculus at the naval postgraduate school in Monterey. Like Sante at the ashram, his knowledge of both physics and spirituality and how it all came together was profound.

LaVon had moved to San Diego to go to college, and she was doing fine. The move did present some challenges for Lisa and Lori.

The high school in Carmel was filled with kids who had few social skills. The first day at school, the girls were looking for their first class. When they asked another student for directions, she looked at them as if they were bugs and stuck her nose in the air as she walked on. This was not a good introduction to a new school.

Our girls were not simply given money; they were required to earn it. They each found a part-time job right after they got there. Kids in Carmel were not required to work, and they looked down on those who did. Back in Incline, they were popular, but here, not so much. The girls were able to find friends from Salinas and Seaside schools, and together they would cruise Main Street in Salinas. Some of the guys from Fort Ord, a military base close by, would also cruise Main Street. There were hundreds of young men in their early twenties from all parts of the country based at Fort Ord. Each girl in the valley had a broad selection of young men to choose from. These relationships would change the girls' lives forever. They were both married by age eighteen, and both started families far too soon.

On the flip side, Jill was improving, and Sundance Development was doing better than I expected, even with my high expectations. The cost breakdown was reasonable, and we were coming in under budget. The construction profit was going to be more than planned.

Units were selling fast enough to raise the price a bit, so profits on the sales were better than expected. If you can raise the sales price on a $100,000 unit by just 2 percent ($2,000) and you have two hundred to sell, you just increased your bottom line by $400,000. That's a nice little extra.

The one thing I did indulge in was flying lessons. Shortly after launching the project, I started studying and taking lessons to fly an airplane. Not only was I going to learn to fly, but I was going to learn to fly in instrument conditions as Jim had on our way to Tucson. As luck would have it, Air Trails, the company I chose to teach me, ran a temp run for the government each morning at five o'clock. It was an instructor's job to fly to five thousand feet and record the temperature at every thousand feet. The instructors were only too happy to let me fly the airplane while they relaxed and did the paperwork. It was foggy more often than not, so I was able to log a fair amount of time and practice a lot of instrument landings in instrument conditions without having to pay. Very few pilots got this kind of actual instrument training.

I will say that learning to fly an airplane when you can see absolutely nothing from the time you leave the runway till you get it back on the ground safely is one of the biggest challenges I ever embarked on, much more so than racing motorcycles. If you mess up controlling the motorcycle, your body may bounce a few times before coming to rest. In fact, I did that on occasion. If you make a mistake flying an airplane in instrument conditions, there is an excellent chance you and everyone with you will die. The first time I flew an airplane solo from an airport where I couldn't see the end of the runway because of the fog, flew it to the next airport in fog so thick that there were no visual references, and landed it safely gave me the greatest sense of accomplishment I could imagine.

Shortly after getting my pilot's license, I started flying Jill to Sedona, Arizona, for the weekend. Actually, we went a lot of other places, but Sedona was a favorite of ours. We had met friends in Carmel who lived in Sedona and had a second home in Carmel-by-the-Sea. They felt splitting their time between the high desert and the ocean was about as good as it could get. Jill and I started talking about setting up something like that in the future.

CHAPTER 18

JILL IS THERE FOR ME

It was 1985, and the construction business could not have been better for me. Month after month, we receive $500,000 in cash flow on the construction side and another $500,000 on the sales of units. All this was going to retire the construction debt as well as other debts sooner than anticipated.

At this point, we could calculate the net results on the financial aspect of this project. We were able to trim construction cost, and as a result, the profits would cover the million in debt as anticipated and provide a couple hundred thousand more. With the increased sales price of the completed units, the net profit on home sales was going to come in closer to two and a half million.

One of the brighter spots in our financial future was the fact that Norm Matson, the man who had referred us to the 250-unit project, owned a factory that was producing a composite material used to create floor, wall, and roof panels for apartment buildings. His system created a living space that was superior in every way to standard construction methods. It was infinitely stronger, would not burn, had an insulation factor unachievable by standard construction, and could be put in place for roughly half the cost of normal stick-built homes. He employed more than three hundred people, and he was running three shifts and producing units 24-7 for 350 days out of the year. The product was called Fibershel.

With our cash flow, we were able to tie up land in Monterey to construct five hundred apartments and another piece of land just north of our existing 250-unit project for a hundred mini storage units.

The Fibershel material would put our five hundred apartments in service at a very favorable cost, and the maintenance would be minimal. We would use the same material for the storage units. We did not use the product on the condo project as it was approved as stick-built, and it would have taken too long to reengineer and get approvals to make the necessary changes. I introduced Mr. Matson to the board of directors of the bank, and they had extended him a line of credit for $20 million. That gave him the ability to negotiate contracts of almost $100 million. I earned a fee for that, a substantial one that I would receive from profits.

We signed papers on a $17-million construction loan for the five hundred units of apartments. The construction time would be short, and the cost would be low because we going to use the product from the factory. The value of the completed project would be in excess of $22 million. Once rented out, the income from the project would retire the debt against the property in less than fifteen years. If all went as planned, Jill and I would have at least five hundred apartments, one hundred storage units, and a nice home at Tahoe paid for before I turned sixty—that is, if we did nothing else for the next fifteen years. We had the wherewithal, and I knew exactly how to make that all happen.

It was time for the second-to-last draw on the second phase of the condo project. It had become my habit to drive to the city to pick up the construction draw. The amount of this check would be a bit more than $497,000. Each month I would give the president of the bank an update not only on the progress of the project but on Jill and the family too. The meeting was never long, but he gave me his undivided attention as he did for all of his bigger clients. He liked to know exactly what was going on, not only with our business but with the people doing the business. He had developed a healthy respect for Jill long before she entered the hospital the first time, and he followed her progress with interest. He had construction management people who watched the project and the cash flow, but these meetings kept him personally in touch.

This day would be etched in my mind as much as any other in my life. When I arrived at the bank, the parking lot was almost empty, and a man was standing at the front door as if on guard.

I asked, "What's going on?"

"This bank is closed," the man responded. "I represent the federal government, and we have taken over."

As I drove home, it was much the same as the drive back over the hill after I left Jill in the hospital with a stroke. I simply thought we would find out why this had happened and fix it. I had no idea what that day really meant in our lives. Health-wise, the magnitude was monumental. Financially, this occurrence would be equally catastrophic.

Through it all, Jill did not let herself get down. She was convinced in her heart that somehow some good would come of this. If we had our health and each other, we would be just fine. During the medical crisis, I was there for Jill. During this economic meltdown, Jill would be there for me.

For a guy, losing a business that brought in $1 million a month with millions in assets and being left with no cash flow, no assets, and a bunch of debt is more than a major setback. The government locked up everything, including all our bank accounts. Because we could not make payments, they foreclosed and took all the properties, including the Castle. We had done absolutely nothing wrong. I was pretty sure no one at the bank had done anything wrong. Time would prove me correct.

I was really ticked off, and there was nothing anyone could do. I knew that these emotions would cause problems sooner or later, but I couldn't help it. I was very angry about the whole thing. This time Jill would pull me through. There was no way she was going to let me wallow in self-pity.

Along with her other studies, Jill had been continually studying metaphysical laws. The term *metaphysical* means "the cause and nature of things." We would discuss these concepts at length, and we found that some of these laws not only made sense but were applicable to us and what had happened in our lives. Moreover, she was finding that with proper application of these laws, predictable outcomes were possible.

We had already experienced in the Philippines one of the seven laws of the universe we had been presented with—*the law of vibration*. This law is mutable, meaning it can be transcended or at least better used. This law says everything in the universe vibrates at a certain frequency. Nothing is solid, not even you. The healers had the ability to raise the frequency at which they normally vibrated and enter the body. We watched it happen and saw and felt the results. It was real to us. It is also the law at the core of the law of attraction, which says that like energy attracts like energy.

A few years later, we would study the teachings of Abraham brought to us by Jerry and Ester Hicks. This was still long before the internet and the CD had had not been invented. The information was recorded on cassette tapes. Today the information is readily available online. The way it is articulated by Abraham the law says, "That witch is like unto itself is drawn." How Ester hears it is exactly the way she states it. It is just another way of saying the same thing. This is the basis of thought power. Without knowing the law, we used it to create an outrageous English Tudor home. Everything starts with a thought. That is why we say, "You cannot afford the luxury of a negative thought."

When we were introduced to the law of mentalism, which is immutable, meaning it cannot be altered, we then understood how the Castle came about. That law says that "everything in the universe that is started with thought." We now understood a bit more about how we created those things we so much wanted in our lives. Understanding the negative or *what we perceived to be negative* would take some time.

Jill decided we were going to focus on what we had, not on what we had lost.

What we did have was our relationship and our health. By this time, Jill was gaining strength and endurance every day. It was not going to come back all at once, but it was coming back. She was getting stronger every day, and with that, she was able to overcome the balance issues caused by her nerve damage. Through her study of natural health and the reasons that a balanced organic diet, proper rest, relaxation, and exercise were so necessary, we both felt good about the direction we were going.

We had a few tools and toys. We had some company trucks, a personal truck and camper, a boat, and a motorcycle that we had paid for. If we sold some of those tools and toys, we could put the money together to move. We decided to do just that as I felt that I needed to go somewhere and hide, think, and heal. The study of metaphysics was helping us, and we wished to go somewhere that would support that study. I had not been studying long enough to understand that I would still be wherever I went, so at the time, moving seemed like the thing to do.

The personal truck and camper were the first to sell. Together they were worth maybe $12,000. I offered them for $10,000. I took $5,000 from the first guy who came up with cash as we really needed the money.

I found a job doing finish work for both me and my son Abe. He had quit school and gone to work for my company, and now he had some ten years of experience as a carpenter. When he was younger, he was not always consistent when it came to showing up for work. He now had a wife and a child to support, so I had high hopes he would settle down. He was one of the best all-around carpenters who had ever worked for me. He had an amazing wife, a wonderful child, and a great attitude. Attitude—now that is a word we need to spend some time on. It was easy to look at my son's situation. He had a great family, time, talent, and a good attitude. With those, a man could accomplish anything. I was only eighteen years older than this chap. If the philosophy is good for him, it should be good for me.

With money from the truck, we rented an airplane and set course for Sedona. In the past, we had flown there on occasion and developed some close friendships. I had not been in the cockpit for a while, and it really felt good. When you are flying an airplane, you don't have time to think of much else, and I did not need to think about what had just happened in my life.

There was a neat motel at the airport in Sedona, and we checked in on a Friday evening. Our plan was to spend the weekend looking for rentals and work. If we moved, the cash from the toys would not last long, and we had no idea what we could expect to pay for rent. We weren't even sure that we could rent anything with little money and no jobs.

The law of deliberate creation says that if you wish to create something, you must get clear in your mind what it is you want to see happen. You must stay focused on it, and you must seize the opportunity to realize your goal when it presents itself. One aspect of this law says that if something does not happen easily, it is likely not the right thing to do. Things in your life should happen easily.

We got up Saturday morning and had breakfast with friends. Breakfast with friends turned into lunch with other friends, and the next thing we knew, we were having dinner with a wonderful group of people. We found ourselves on our way back to the motel after a wonderful day, but we had done no research. We had not looked for a rental place or jobs. We could only stay until Sunday night as I had to go to work installing cabinets on Monday morning.

When we returned to the motel, Jill picked up a paper in the office, and we went to our room. There was one house for rent in the paper. It was almost too late to call, but I called anyway. A young girl answered the phone. She sounded like she was in her early teens, and I had a fascinating talk with a most delightful child. I found she was in fact thirteen, but our conversation revealed she was wise far beyond her years. She explained that her parents were working late every evening on their new home. She knew they planned to put in a long day tomorrow since they were all anxious to get the new home finished. She made an appointment for us to meet her folks early the next day, Sunday, see the house, and talk with her parents.

We got up early and went straight to the address we had been given. The young lady had given us excellent directions. We were expecting a short meeting and a tour of the house before breakfast. The short meeting we expected turned into spending an entire day with newfound friends. We shared two meals, stories of miracles, philosophy about metaphysical truths, time in meditation, some laughter, and even some tears.

At the end of it, I said, "Let me get my checkbook."

"No need for that," the man said. "You go back to California and wrap things up, and the house will be ready for you when you get here. We'll hold it for you. It's yours."

Talk about validation. This was fun, and it was easy. Not only had we fallen in love with Sedona, which was not a hard thing to do, but we also loved everyone we met there. On top of it all, we had found a very nice home. The only thing between the house and famous Bell Rock was a little bit of high Arizona desert.

We decided to have dinner before we set course for Carmel. The airport had a nice restaurant, and over dinner we talked about the past two days and how much we enjoyed the people we already knew in Sedona.

Jill began, "We have some really good friends here. It's a small town, and it's beautiful, one of the most beautiful places I've ever seen. This area has the same intrigue for me as it did when I was a child."

"It's the same feeling I have when I'm high in the Sierras," I said. "I love the way it feels here too, and I know this is a very special place. However, I know in my heart I am not going to be happy if Hawaii is not part of our life, and my vision is still crystal clear. In that vision of running on the beach, we were living there, not visitors. I am not through with Incline Village either. I still love that place and our friends there."

"Remember our discussions about splitting our time between Sedona and the ocean?" Jill asked.

"Yes, I do. Why? What are you thinking?"

"Well, at the time we were thinking maybe Sedona and Carmel, right?"

"Yes, I'm listening."

"Well, if Sante was right—and I believe he was—God wants for us what we want for us. If we wish to split our time between here and Kailua and maybe keep a home in Incline too, all we have to do is get clear about what it is we want and watch for the opportunities. When they present themselves, we go for them."

We knew that we wanted to spend time in Hawaii, to be in business for ourselves, and to build a fine English Tudor home, and all those came to be faster and grander than we could have imagined. Our stated desire to spend time in Hawaii resulted in a move there. The Tudor home ended up as a five-thousand-square-foot castle, and the business we started quickly grew to an enterprise much larger than envisioned. We never put forth any restrictions on ourselves. We just never lost the vision, and we acted on the opportunities when they presented themselves.

"I like what you're saying, Jill. Where do you think the money will come from for all this?"

There it was again, that look, the one that says, "Aren't you ever going to get it?"

She replied, "I know in my heart and soul our medical challenges are a thing of the past for this lifetime. We could never in a million years have been able to imagine the Philippine healers. We were forced to turn it all over to God, right?"

"You're right there. Go on."

"Our financial condition looked grim when we returned from Baguio City, don't you agree?"

"It did."

"If we've learned one thing through all this, it's to have faith in God and complete trust that we will be taken care of. So I suggest faith and trust."

"It is really that simple for you, isn't it?"

"It is that simple."

"All right, darling wife of mine, I can't argue that one. Count me in."

We would move to Sedona, Arizona, to heal—physically, emotionally, and spiritually—and to learn to meditate, to reflect, and to study metaphysical laws.

When you're flying west in the evening, a sunset can last for what seems like forever. That evening I flew that rented Piper PA-28 into a never-ending sunset. We both knew that all illness was in our past. We had each other, and we had our health. With those, we could accomplish whatever we wished. Tomorrow the sun would rise again, this time on a whole new chapter in our lives. This new fresh start would start in Sedona, Arizona, a perfect place to continue the study of metaphysics.

Flying that Piper PA-28 west into a never-ending sunset

CHAPTER 19

MORE HEALING, MORE STUDY

In order to fund the move to Sedona, I sold the blue jet boat, my street bike, all but one set of tools, and pretty much every asset left—all personal, nothing the company owned. The government took everything, including all bank accounts and all property. We decided not to sue the federal government. We had friends who lost much more than we did and followed that route. They found that a federal judge will never rule against the federal government no matter what the evidence. I had worked twenty-five years to build what we had, and it was gone. In a way, this was as big a setback for me as Jill's health issues were for her. We had seen the law of rhythm in action. This law basically says that as the pendulum swings one way, it is bound to swing the other. The degree to which it swings simply depends on how far it was forced to go in the first direction. The measure of the swing one way is the measure of the swing the other. This law is also mutable. Everything in life ebbs and flows. When it is swinging in the wrong direction, turn it all over to God. Be sure God knows what it is you want to manifest. In this life, occasionally bad things happen to good people. By this time we knew that how we reacted to the events in our life is all important.

The turn of events in Salinas was not going to define us; we were going to come back stronger.

Jill was learning to really listen to her intuition. Prior to the stroke, she knew that at some level, our life was out of balance. She was trying to be everything to everyone. She was bent on being the best mother, the best wife, the best realtor, the best housekeeper, the best friend, etc., and she left nothing for herself. I was far too focused on making a living and not focused at all on making a life. In Sedona, we would focus more on making a life and Jill on taking care of Jill. We still had in mind living part-time in Sedona and part-time at the ocean. Just how and when was not up to us.

We had no idea God was setting us up when we became friends and study partners in these laws of the universe with a couple about our age whom we had met early in our stay in Carmel. Kavanagh and Rochelle had escaped from LA and had a home in Carmel. Some time prior to the government relieving us of all our assets, our friends whom we referred to as K and R had moved to the south of France. We stayed in touch. They called one day just after we made the decision to move to Sedona. They informed us that living in France was not working as they had anticipated and that they were coming back to the good old United States. When we asked where, they said, "We really do not know. We are trying to figure that out."

I said, "We are in the process of packing to move to Sedona. We have a nice three-bedroom home waiting for us, and we would be happy to share that until you figure it out."

They answered, "Sounds perfect." We set up a schedule so that they could meet us there the day we arrived. They would help us move in.

The drive from Carmel on the coast of California to Sedona is usually about fifteen hours. When we left Carmel, I was driving a moving van with Jill's car on a trailer in tow. Jill was driving my truck with a big trailer behind that. As things went, the rented truck did not have the power to haul the load we had. It was slow. Jill and I drove twenty-six hours straight through. We did not stop for sleep, just food and bathroom breaks. Jill was certainly improving. We were a day late getting to Sedona.

K and R arrived on time and met the owner of the home, and they had become friends by the time we arrived. I had not had the opportunity to tell the owner we were going to share the house, but he took it all in stride. He also agreed to let us repaint the interior to suit our décor, which we did prior to moving all the furniture in. We got it all done, moved in, arranged our stuff, and took a day to explore Sedona. During our first real dinner at home, the phone rang.

"Howsit? You busy?" It was that familiar Japanese Hawaiian voice. It was my friend Misau. He asked me if I could come to Hawaii to help build a large home on Oahu. He needed me for at least three months just to frame the house, longer if I did the electrical system and helped finish it. This home was some five thousand square feet. He told me he was working on the plans to bid the construction of a home more than three times the size of this one. Because of his contacts, the project would be ours if we wanted it. The cost of construction would be more than ten million dollars.

K and R agreed to take care of everything in Sedona, including our dog. As it worked out, we stayed for six months during this trip, and it worked out for all concerned. K and R had not planned to stay that long, but they also made the decision to let go and let God. By the time we returned, they had decided to stay in Sedona and were ready to establish a home of their own. They each had a good income and a wide circle of friends. When we returned, they moved into their own home.

Jill and I found Sedona to be everything we expected and more. We loved living there. It was to become a home base for the next ten years. During those years we not only spent a great deal of time in Hawaii, (up to a year at a time) but also established a home in Incline Village. It was what we envisioned, and it was delicious.

CHAPTER 20

DENNIS—A GREAT TEACHER

Jill's parents were living in Carson City, Nevada, and mine were still in the foothills on the western side of the Sierra Nevada Mountains. Neither was far from Tahoe, and we also had close friends we felt a need to see in Incline Village. For those reasons, we would make periodic trips north. The trip from Sedona would take fifteen to sixteen hours to drive, and my preference was to leave after dinner, drive straight through, and get to our destination on the following day. After a short nap when we arrived, I could get in a full day in each location. On occasion we would drive about halfway, spend the night in southern Nevada, and complete the trip on the second day. We met Dennis on one of these trips.

It was February, and we got up early in Las Vegas. We had come from Carson City and made it as far as Vegas and spent the night. I had planned to drive straight through, but for some reason pulled into a motel and checked in. Las Vegas is not my favorite town, and I would not normally stay there. I had no idea why I stopped there. I just turned in and checked in.

Winters in southern Nevada can be very cold. It was below freezing when we left our hotel that morning. In good weather this leg of the trip would take five to six hours with stops for fuel and food. It would be snowing when we reached Flagstaff, and it was better to drive through a snowstorm in the midday if possible, so we left early.

Not too far east of Vegas, we would pass through the town of Bolder. As we were leaving Bolder, we noticed a young man standing by the road with his thumb out, trying to hitch a ride. He wore sneakers, Levis, and a short-sleeved shirt—nothing to protect himself against the bitter cold. I had done a fair amount of hitchhiking as a lad, so now I rarely passed a person who needed a lift. This was a practice that left Jill a bit uncomfortable at times, but this time she never raised an eyebrow. It never occurred to me not to stop for this guy. All he had for luggage was a small bag. He was a nice-looking chap who was maybe in his mid-thirties. His clothes were worn thin but clean. He was sincerely appreciative to be inside where it was warm.

"What's your destination?" I asked.

"Uhhh ... Phoenix," he said almost as a question.

"So what takes you to Phoenix?"

Again, he paused. "I hope warmth and work. Las Vegas is really cold, and I couldn't find a job there, only a day's work here and there."

"What kind of work do you do?"

"I like landscaping. I'd like to work as a landscaper."

"So are you really warm-blooded, or do you not have a coat?"

"I had one, but someone stole it. I was staying in a shelter last night, and when I awoke, it was gone."

"So what made you decide to hitchhike out of town without a coat?"

"I was kind of hoping you wouldn't ask me that," he said. "It's sort of a weird story."

"Have you got a name?"

"It's Dennis. Dennis Williams."

"Okay, Dennis, we're not going all the way to Phoenix, but we're going as far as Sedona. That's just a bit more than a hundred miles short of Phoenix. From here to Sedona is six to eight hours, depending on how much snow we encounter, so we've got plenty of time to hear your story."

The truck was a single cab with one seat. With Jill, the dog, and I as well as Dennis now, it was a bit tight, but the dog stretched out on Jill and Dennis.

The trip to Flagstaff took most of the day, and during the drive we got a detailed account of the past fifteen years of his life with snippets of his childhood. We learned how he came to be standing by the road in Bolder, Nevada.

It seems that our new friend Dennis was from New Jersey. His mom had him very late in life, and she was now in her late seventies. His father had passed away long ago.

Dennis had been married and had his own business delivering pharmaceutical products on the East Coast. The business took a great deal of his time, a fact that his new wife could not cope with. She gave him an ultimatum. He would spend more time with her ... or else.

In an effort to show her what a poor demand she had made, he sold his business to a competitor for a dollar, so his wife left him.

He had a friend who owned a bar, so he got a job bartending. He was good at it, but he did not like the clients the business drew and wished to work outdoors. So he went to work for a client of the bar in the landscape business. He loved it. He could see where this business could be most profitable and fulfill his desire to be outdoors. As time passed, the man kept coming up short on pay.

At first, this was confusing, as he knew his boss had lucrative contracts. He later came to realize that the man had a gambling problem and all the money was going to the New Jersey casinos.

In talking with others in the business, he was told that if he really wanted to make money in the landscape business, he should go to California. There he could work year-round, and the money was better. So that's what he decided to do. From there, things started really going downhill.

He had an acquaintance who was planning a trip to LA and who had agreed to take Dennis with him. So Dennis sold what was left after the divorce, which wasn't much, sold his car for what he owed on it, and got ready to move. The driver of his free ride decided not to go, but Dennis was going anyway. He found a truck driver who was heading for the West Coast and agreed to take him along. The truck was bound for the state of Washington, but that was close enough for him. He could hitchhike down the West Coast to LA.

He had no idea what a long, time-consuming, and expensive task that would be. He did, however, make it to LA. He had been told he could sleep on the beach until he found an apartment or a room. That option ended almost immediately, as a peace officer ushered him off the beach and told him where he could find a shelter. So a homeless shelter was where he spent his first night in California as he would have to conserve what little money he had.

When he awoke in the morning, every last thing he owned was gone. He had no clothes other than what he was wearing, no wallet, no money, no ID, nothing.

Just outside the shelter, a man who seemed friendly enough pulled his car to a stop and said, "You look a little lost. Do you need some help?"

"That's an understatement," Dennis said. "I need food, and I need work. And I need both real soon."

"Hop in. Maybe I can help."

They went to a beautiful home where the nice man prepared a hearty breakfast. No sooner had Dennis finished his meal than the supposedly nice man made his true intentions known. Dennis had heard of this kind of fellow, but he was not prepared for the action this guy had in mind. He bolted from the house and ran until he could run no more.

He was able to get to a shelter that night and went to bed hungry. In conversation with other homeless people, he was told there was a blood bank where he could get ten dollars for his blood. His options were few. He was too proud to call his mother, determined to figure his life out on his own. When he got to the blood bank, he saw most of the donors looked pretty old and pretty used up.

He asked, "Isn't my blood worth more than these people's? I'm young and healthy."

"Ten dollars. Take it or leave it," they answered.

It did not take long to figure out that you can't get a job if you don't have an address. If you don't have an address, you can't get a job. It took some time, but he determined the hunt for a job in LA would be futile. He was told that in Las Vegas, anyone could work in the casinos. Los Angeles and the people he found there left a bad taste in his mouth. He would hitch a ride to Vegas.

In Las Vegas, he found a shelter much like the one in LA. What he hadn't figured on was the cold. While in LA, he had procured a few essentials, including a toothbrush and other toiletries and also a jacket. Vegas afforded him some day jobs, but nothing that would ever get him an apartment. He was living with vagrants, and he was treated like one. The longer this went on, the worse he felt about himself. He was past ashamed to call his mother. He simply couldn't.

Thoughts of suicide entered his head, and the more he entertained the idea, the better the option sounded. With the proceeds from a day's labor, he was able to purchase a pistol from another homeless person. He planned to end it all, but he couldn't. He said, "If you want to know what a total failure is, become homeless, plan to kill yourself, and fail at that."

Then he said, "Now we're back to the part where you asked me why I left Las Vegas with no coat. I told you it was a rather weird story. I woke up this morning to an audible voice that said, 'Leave this city now.' Everyone else was gone or asleep. When I found my jacket was missing, I thought, *I can't leave*. The voice said, 'Leave at once. You do not need the jacket.' There was no question in my mind that I was supposed to leave. I left the shelter and got an immediate ride to Bolder. They were nice people who lived there and dropped me off right where you picked me up. I hope you don't think I'm crazy. The voice was audible to me. It was loud and clear."

We assured him that we did not think he was crazy.

Jill and I always carry veggies and healthy munchies with us, so we shared those with Dennis and drove through lunchtime. We got to Flagstaff in the late afternoon, as we had encountered snow a considerable distance west of town. Flagstaff is at 7,500 feet in elevation and when we arrived, it was snowing heavily, a wet and cold snow. The first stop was the buffet at Sizzler. Our son Abe was tall and thin, and Dennis had the same build. We were always amazed at the amount of food Abe could consume at one sitting. Dennis had about the same build and was also able to consume a lot of fuel at one time. It took considerable time to fill him up, and that was okay.

Our next stop was the Army-Navy surplus store where we knew we would find a good coat, a scarf for his neck, and gloves. Next we bought some healthy munchies that would fit in the oversize pockets of his new army jacket.

Ordinarily, we would drive down Oak Creek Canyon to Sedona. The road down the canyon was narrow and steep with hairpin curves. In a major snowstorm, this would not be the best route anyway.

Either way, we planned to take Dennis to the intersection of Highway 179 and US 17 south of Sedona and drop him off. US 17 was a major freeway that went all the way to Phoenix, which was another hundred miles or so. We drove down US 17 to Highway 179, where we would turn north to Sedona. It was snowing heavily.

"Dennis, I think you'd better spend the night with us. It's too dark and too cold to dump you out here."

What was he going to say? He couldn't refuse and tell us to leave him here on the road in the freezing cold." It was pretty dark and snowing when we reached our home in Sedona. It was early enough, and we had already had what could be considered dinner, so we talked long into the night. We found him to be very likable.

We shared with him some of the laws of metaphysics, and we gave him information about how he may change what was going on in his life through the laws. He was more than receptive and wanted to know what we knew and how we had come to know these things. He had been raised Catholic but had never followed the religion. It was very late when we finally retired for the evening after spending considerable time on mentalism, the law of deliberate creation, and the law of attraction, which all had a lot to do with the law of rhythm.

Jill and I have lived in some of the most beautiful places. Sedona, Arizona, is at the top of the list. If you took a hundred people to the Nevada City-Grass Valley area, Hawaii, Lake Tahoe, Carmel, and Sedona, they would all likely take more pictures of Sedona than anywhere else. It is beautiful, especially after a snowstorm. Sometime before daybreak the storm cleared, and in the morning the sky looked very blue in contrast to the red rock with white snow. When Dennis arose and looked outside, he could not believe that what he was looking at was real. He had no idea that this kind of natural beauty existed. What he was looking at was as pretty as any place on earth. The morning was spectacular.

We had a leisurely breakfast and talked about where Sedona was in the world physically and spiritually and what made it so special. Dennis was like a child seeing Disneyland for the first time. When we arose that morning, we intended to drop him off on US 17 bound for Phoenix with his thumb out.

As the conversation unfolded, I said, "You know what? You're right. If you do not have an address, it is almost impossible to find a job. If you don't have a job, you cannot get an address."

I looked at Jill, and she knew what I was asking. Without saying a word, she agreed. I went on. "Per capita, there are likely as many opportunities here as there are in Phoenix. You only need one position. I suspect that if you use this as an address, you may find that position. Are you up for sticking around?"

We really thought we could make a profound difference in this young man's life. We also felt that in twenty-four hours we knew him pretty well. We did not perceive him to be a risk. His words and emotional response made us glad we had made the offer.

It was truly a profound experience for all concerned. Next we called K and R and gave them a rundown. As Dennis was about the same size as our friend back from France, we thought we might fit him with a change of clothes. When we arrived at their home, Dennis was greeted as if he were an old friend. As luck would have it, the two guys were almost the exact same size. When we departed, Dennis had a suitcase full of work clothes, street clothes, nice clothes, several pairs of shoes, and a new sweat suit. He was completely unprepared for the love, acceptance, and generosity. I think he sensed his four new friends were having about as much fun as they could have. We exchanged hugs and words of encouragement as we left K and R's house.

When we got back into the truck, I explained to Dennis that the main street, the only commercial street in Sedona, ran east and west. I was going to drop him off at the east end of town, and he was to walk the south side of the street, stopping at every business to put in an application if they would accept one. I gave him some money for lunch and a phone call and told him to call me once that was done or if he got a job. Late that afternoon he called from the west end of town. He'd had had an interesting day, but he hadn't found a job. He had met more warm and concerned people than he could have imagined. What he did get from everyone was that it was February. Sedona is totally a tourist town, and this was not tourist season.

"My God, these people are different from the ones in LA or Vegas. For that matter, they're not much like New Jersey people either," he said. "I liked everyone I met."

"We like the folks here too. They all seem to have a keen awareness that what goes around comes around. It's fun to be around people who are living their lives on purpose. We feel fortunate to live here."

That evening we had a great dinner. Other friends came over and talked late into the night. Dennis made a great first impression on everyone.

The next morning when Dennis got up, he said, "It happened again—the voice. I'm supposed to meet Jerry."

"Is that all you got?" I asked. "Just Jerry?"

"I take it you don't know a Jerry."

"Not offhand. We'll have to see what unfolds. Let's head for the east end of town again. This time you can walk the north side of the street."

He leaned back in his chair with his hands locked behind his head, smiled, and said, "It's time to call my mother and let her know I'm okay." After he returned from the call, I asked how it went. "She wanted to know if I was free to leave if I wished. She said she had heard of people like I described and it worried her."

"Let's go find you a job so you can fly back and see her."

This time he dressed in a white shirt and black pants, which made him look anything but homeless. It was late afternoon when Dennis made it almost to the west end of town. He stopped in at a restaurant called the Coffee Pot, a breakfast, lunch, and dinner place with a bar on one side. All he had noticed was the sign that said, "Home of 101 Omelets." When he asked the lady at the reception desk if they were hiring, she said, "No, it's our slow season, you know. If you wish, you can take an application and drop it by when you've completed it."

"Would it be okay if I filled it out right here?"

"Of course. The bar isn't open yet. Just take a stool at the bar over there."

He was almost finished with the application when a guy slid up on the stool beside him. The man asked, "Can I look at your application?"

"Sure, if you wish."

"Ah, I see you have experience tending bar."

"Yes, I do," Dennis said. "I had fun when I did it, so I was pretty good at it."

The man said, "My name is Jerry. I'm the owner here, and I could use a bartender. When could you be available?"

185

"Your name's really Jerry?"

"Yes, it's Jerry. Did you miss the sign outside?"

Dennis must have had a disbelieving or at least an astonished look on his face, so Jerry said, "Come on outside. I can't believe you missed it."

They went out front, and there it was as big as life: "Jerry's Coffee Pot Restaurant, Home of 101 Omelets."

"Well, you look as though you're dressed okay for the job. Let's go in and get you an apron, and we can open this place up right now."

"May I make a phone call first? I have to call my ride."

"Sure, go right ahead."

When I picked Dennis up late that night, he had tip money in his pocket. He worked with Jerry all evening, and they both had a great time. What Dennis could not get over was the profound difference in the bar crowd. These folks were locals having deep philosophical conversations about spiritual things over drinks and having a genuinely good time at it. These people were happy even before they got to the bar. The crowd he had served back East came to drown their sorrows. Some of the conversations made him think the voice he had been hearing was not so strange after all. Not much like the normal bar crowd, these patrons were learning to live their lives on purpose and sharing with others how it was all going.

He told me on the way home he had never in his life felt so content and excited about the future. We talked about where he had been in his life just a couple days earlier and how fast things can turn around. He was more than anxious to learn everything he could about living life on purpose and how to create a life you design.

Dennis was a blank slate to work with, and work with him we did. Life for him was going to get very good very fast. We knew a young lady a couple years younger than Dennis, and we were anxious for them to meet. I had no idea how he would react when he met her. She was completely autonomous. She was pretty but wore little or no makeup. She spent a great deal of time with or on her horse, and she ate nothing but raw food. She had her own business, had a lot of friends, one of whom was Jill, and was not really looking for a man in her life. It would take a pretty special man to catch her attention. When Lynn came by the house and met Dennis, I could tell there were no sparks flying in either direction.

At about this time our youngest, Lori, called from California and informed us she was getting married to Steve the following weekend in Las Vegas. They had decided to do this no matter what; however, they wished for us to be there. Lori had moved to Southern California with Steve, one of the servicemen from Fort Ord, prior to our moving to Sedona. Of course, we decided to go to Las Vegas to attend the wedding. Even though we had only known Dennis for about two weeks, we asked him to watch the house and the dog while we went to Vegas. He could use the truck for work. All I asked was that it be clean and full of fuel when we returned.

We left for Las Vegas early Saturday, attended the wedding that evening, stayed through Sunday, and drove home Monday. When we returned, the house was spotless, the truck clean and filled with gas, and Dennis had made some new friends. All had indeed gone well. He also spent a fair amount of time talking with Lynn over the weekend, as she had come by not knowing we would be gone.

A couple weeks later, he confided in me, "I knew what you had in mind when you introduced me to Lynn, and I thought, *These well-intentioned folks have no idea about my taste in women.* The more time I spend with her, the more fascinated I am. I find I wish to be around her as much as I can, and this has nothing to do with physical attraction. I think I want her as a friend. This has never happened to me before. I think we are simply going to be very good friends and nothing more, which makes no sense to me. I'll give you this. She is a very wise young lady. I think that somehow makes her more attractive, but I am okay with having her as a good friend. I really like talking with her."

Speaking of good friends, Dennis had told us he'd always had a fascination with Native Americans. Where he had come from there were few of these folks. In Sedona, Arizona, it was not all that uncommon to find people with that heritage. It had not taken long for him to strike up a friendship with a real Native American. He was a young man who was recently divorced just as Dennis was, and his divorce also left him little in the way of worldly assets.

Jesse, the new friend, was living with his parents. He and Dennis had been talking about getting an apartment and sharing the expenses. They both wanted to be independent, and this would be a big step in that direction. Jess worked at Enchantment, an upscale resort just outside Sedona, and he knew everyone in town. It was through one of these contacts that Dennis landed a second job waiting tables at Los Abrigados, one of the nicest places in Sedona. A good waiter there could make excellent money. He was paying his own way, but he needed to step up the income to get a car and an apartment of his own. We didn't mind him living with us at all. It was so much fun to watch him grow. Not only was he open to learning new things, but he was more than ready act on what he was learning too. When you meditate at a vortex in Sedona (or anywhere else for that matter), communication is enhanced. Dennis spent time in meditation, and with nature. He determined his landscape work had filled him with a need to spent time with nature. Lynn would take him on long hikes to some of the best spots around Sedona, places the locals knew about.

Not only was he pleasant to have around, but he was also a big help. We would take long hikes and have in-depth conversations. And he was beginning to think his relationship with a certain young lady may progress to another level soon. At one point he said, "I am not going to go as far as to say the word love, but it's awfully strong like."

During this time Dennis and I were part of a black-tie event in town together. It was a high-end fashion show, and I was the master of ceremonies while Dennis ushered the ladies to the stage. The event was a huge success, and we enjoyed doing it. Lynn was one of the models, and with makeup and the high-dollar clothes, she was just stunning. It was obvious she was very much enjoying being on his arm.

A little more than a month after Lori's wedding, we got a call from our now married youngest. They wanted us to come to San Diego, where they had moved when we left for Sedona, and celebrate with their friends. This was not only a marriage reception but a celebration of the possibility of our third grandchild. We wouldn't have missed it. It would have been our wish that they wait until the relationship was a bit more seasoned to have a child, but what do parents know?

Again, Dennis agreed to care for the house and the truck. This time we would take the dog with us, as he would be working two jobs and long hours. He would buy that car and rent that apartment in the very near future. Actually, Dennis had agreed to drive to Lake Havasu to see Lynn's parents because her father was ill with cancer and she needed to be there soon. However, since he was scheduled to start a new job, Dennis simply could not leave.

The entire weekend was great fun. Jill and I have always enjoyed long drives together, and we never run out of things to talk about. It also gives us a chance to listen to tapes by our favorite spiritual teachers. All in all, it was a wonderful weekend. The thought of another grandchild was pleasing to both of us. We were not so sure about the relationship, but they were happy and thought they were ready. All we could do was give them love and support, which wasn't really a hard thing to do.

We rolled back into Sedona late Sunday evening. Something was wrong. The truck was there, but it did not look as though it had moved. There were dirty dishes, half-empty cups of coffee, work clothes laid out, and things left as though he'd left in a hurry. It sort of looked as if he'd been abducted. There was no note, nothing. It was just eerie.

We called both his places of employment. Neither had seen him, even though he was scheduled at both. We called friends, but no one knew anything. We knew something was very wrong, but we could not imagine what. We went to bed that night, hoping for answers by the morning. We had very restless night. The sun came up, and nothing had changed. We made phone calls to everyone who might know something and got no answers. I was in the middle of a project, and Jill had appointments with therapeutic massage clients. We decided to give it a day. I went to work, as I didn't know just what else to do. Jill worked out of the house and would be there anyway.

The day at work did nothing to ease my mind. We had sort of adopted Dennis as you would a child. He had become a big part of our lives and the lives of our friends. Jill and I had decided that if he had not returned that evening, we would try the county sheriff. Sedona was not yet incorporated, so there were no police. I really did not want to have to make the call. I knew what was in Dennis's heart, so all we could imagine was foul play, which made no sense at all. I didn't want to dial the number, but I had to. If that was it, I didn't want to hear it. But what else could have happened?

The sheriff himself answered. I explained who I was and said, "I know a person has to be missing for three days to make a missing person's report, but I have a real dilemma."

I explained our relationship to Dennis and why I could not wait three days. His response sent chills down my spine.

He said, "You may have the answer to a puzzle I have. I have a John Doe in the morgue and have had no luck at all with any identification."

"How did this man die?" I asked.

"He was one of two men in a single-car accident on the road that leads to Enchantment. Both were ejected, and both were pronounced dead at the scene. Our John Doe was wearing a sweat suit with no pockets and no ID on him or in the truck. I have a picture. I can bring it over and see if we have a match."

I asked if we could meet at Irene's Restaurant as my wife did not need to be present. He agreed.

I looked at the picture of Dennis for a long time. He was stretched out on a stainless steel tray at the morgue.

I asked, "Was the other man's name Jesse?"

"As a matter of fact, it was."

After confirming his John Doe was in fact our friend Dennis, the sheriff asked how he could contact the man's next of kin. I told him I had his mother's number at the house.

"Do you just want to call her and tell her?" I asked.

"No, from her number we can get an address, and our department will contact the department where she lives. That way someone will be with her when she hears. It's normal to send two officers in a case like this, one male and one female."

"I'll call you with the information," I said.

Back at the house, I walked in, and Jill knew immediately. I think she already knew. I didn't have to say a word. Nor did she. I told her what I knew. "Let's meditate on this for a while and see if we can get some answers, okay?"

We both realized that Dennis had come into our lives as one of the most profound teachers we would ever encounter. He had made a huge impact on us, all our friends, and others he met. He had been raised Catholic, but he had never practiced the religion, so he did not have a lot of religious baggage. Everything we introduced was new to him. We had not been studying metaphysics all that long, just a few years, but this was absolute validation how the laws work.

Dennis was bright, clean, kind, caring, and conscientious, and he had a great work ethic and all the other attributes a couple would like their child to have. He was in his mid-thirties and yet childlike in many ways. He had no idea that he could create a new and different realty in his life by simply changing his thoughts. With enough emotion, the process can take less time, and this young man stated what he wished to see happen and was very emotional about it. He died very suddenly, but at the time he was not only happy with his life, but felt content with what his future held too. He knew that if he did not like something about the direction, he could change it.

Jill had been to church a few times with friends, but she never really studied any one religion, so she was able to digest these things much faster. Her studies of the teachings of Christ on love and healing tied into metaphysics. Our studies were helping us deal with the ups and downs in life. This was definitely one of those downs.

We opted not to get torn up about it. The accident had already happened, and there was nothing that we could do about it now. We also decided that Jill would tell Lynn, who had just returned that morning, and that I would call others.

When Jill entered Lynn's office, she said, "Let's sit down. I have something to tell you."

Just looking at Jill, Lynn knew it was not good. "Is it Gabe?"

" No, Dennis, he was in a car accident and both he and Jesse passed__"

She interrupted, "He died early last Saturday, didn't he?"

"Yes, how did you know?"

"I felt it. I didn't totally understand what I felt till now. We'd connected on a deep spiritual level. I will go up on our mountain and say goodbye." And she left.

That evening we received a call from his mother in New Jersey. She said, "I will come to Sedona. I need to see for myself. They want me to send dental records for positive identification. I am so sure there has been a mistake. I will come myself."

I said, "Please do. You will be welcome in our home."

Dennis had told me about his two sisters. He had never really connected with the elder one. He did not dislike her. He said she was not an easy person to get to know. The younger one, Val, was sweet and simple. He had great affection for her, but he had never really known how to tell her, let alone show her. After he'd been with us and our friends in Sedona, he knew how to do both and was anxious to do just that.

When his mother and sister Val arrived, Jill agreed to take them to the morgue in Flagstaff. His mother was in total denial and had to see for herself. She was not there to see her son. She was sure this was all some horrible mistake. Jill was able to get the ladies through the viewing and back to our home. On the nightstand by his bed, there was a card that he had written to his sister but not yet sent.

My dearest sister Val,

I have loved you all my life. I did not know how to show you. I did not even know how to tell you. I now know how to do both. The next time I see you, you will know for sure your brother loves you. I have learned how to hug those I love. I am looking forward to giving you the biggest hug ever. For now, know I am very happy and content, just know that I do love you.

Your brother,
Dennis

I took a long walk with Val that night and told her everything I knew about her brother. She knew he had never been fond of dogs and had always been afraid the dark. She was pleased to know he loved to take long walks at night with a dog that he loved. I think she knew he'd completed his mission here. Before they left, they made arrangements to have his body flown to New Jersey for a proper burial.

During their stay with us, a number of friends came by. They all knew and loved Dennis, and they were able to tell his mom and Val how he had affected their lives. They all had good things to say, and warm hugs were part of the communication.

His mom later told us that all the hugs she and Val got in Sedona were passed on in New Jersey. His family and friends had never been into big hugs before. Nor had they been comfortable telling people they loved them.

"We do it now," she said. "And we like it. We thank you and your friends in Sedona for that. Your love for one another and your ability to share your love is something Dennis had tried to tell me about. The only way to understand it was to experience it. I understand now what he was trying to tell me." A short time later, we received a package with a set of coffee mugs that had the word "Hugs" on them. We still have them. Jill and I will always be grateful to Dennis for sharing his last days on this earth with us. It has been well over three decades now, and on occasion I still haul out that old military jacket from the Army Navy surplus store in Flagstaff and take a walk with Dennis. We loved him like a son.

To be continued.

EPILOGUE

As I write these words, it has been more than three and a half decades since we visited the healers, and today my beautiful wife lives in perfect health. She never has a bad day. Jill is still working on having a body that will operate perfectly as there is some residual nerve damage, but her health—mental, spiritual, and physical—is perfect. She has a wonderful attitude about whatever happens in life, and she knows that all illness in this lifetime is in her past. When problems arise, she will immediately find some positive aspect in the situation.

From the time we moved to Sedona and for the next thirty years, we spent a great deal of time in Hawaii. Jill found that the people at the women's gym there became like family and helped her build strength. Overcoming a lack of equilibrium comes with strength. Ultimately, she went to work at the gym, teaching others to use the equipment. The women's gym on the mainland is still a big part of her life. She loves working out as it keeps her trim and strong. These attributes go long way toward being healthy and happy witch is a great gift to give the ones in your life that you love. She is still appreciative every morning when she can roll out of bed and stand up by herself.

Later on Jill and I took in three more girls who call us Mom and Dad. So at this point in time, we have ten grandchildren and six great-grandchildren, the youngest of which is my namesake, "Gabriel". We are affectionately known as Tutu Jill (Tutu in Hawaiian means grandmother) and Papa Gabe.

The vision, the one I had the first night in Tucson all those years ago, has become a reality. We have run on Kailua Beach. I was told we would have grandchildren and great-grandchildren, and we certainly do. As I look back on it, the whole thing was an incredible learning experience.

The love we share is not something one can put into words. It never occurred to me to leave her side, not for one minute. After four and a half decades of marriage, I am the winner, and she sees to it that I stay healthy. We would not be who we are now if all this had not happened. It is my plan to sit on Kailua Beach when I reach a hundred, healthy enough to make another bucket list.

My fiftieth birthday party was a total surprise, held at the home of Jerry and Penny McCulloch next door to the castle. Our friends Mac and Marilyn from next door on Kaha St. in Hawaii and Roy were in attendance. Team mates from the motorcycle-racing days, folks from the San Francisco Bay area, and the Mother Lode region in California also were in attendance.

The year 1992, my fiftieth birthday with my best
friends and business partners, Jill and Roy

October 27, 1992, back to Incline Village. The greatest gift
you can give the ones you love is to be happy and healthy.

Splitting our time between Hawaii and Incline
Village again—October 27, 2002

We have seen our exes at family functions over the years, and we are pleased that they have found their own happiness.

We wish to extend our personal thanks and deep gratitude to a few of the people who were a part of our lives as this life changing event unfolded. In no particular order: Dick and Joanne MacDonnell, Jerry and Penny McColloch, Nancy Henderson, Jim Minesh, Georgia McGregor, Marcie Johnson, Marie Loaches, Mac and Marilyn McDermott, Roy Takishita, Linda Harmer, Joy Mae Bowlus, Dennis Williams and Lynn Thomas The private nursing agency in Reno and in particular, Betty, Dr. Jerry Girodano and his staff at the clinic in Tucson as well as the staff at Eldorado Hospital, the real-estate community in Incline Village, the healers, teachers and staff in Bagio City, our families and in particular Jill's sister Pam, my brother Dan and our daughters LaVon, Lisa and Lori. Jill would like to acknowledge Twin Lakes College of the Healing Arts in Santa Cruse and in particular Master Yoo. I would like to acknowledge the president of the bank Ken Kidwell and his staff who will be a major part of the sequel.

.

As I stated previously, it is a lot better to avoid the illness in the first place than to try to rid the body of it after you have allowed the illness a foothold. War on anything or fighting is never the answer. Love is always the answer. Start by learning to love yourself.

It is our plan to travel and to give talks and workshops on living a healthy lifestyle. We can be contacted on the Web at GabrielRichardsCommunications.com or by email at jillandgabe.com

Giving Love a Voice, book two, which covers lessons in money, is next. In the meantime, let us study together how to be healthy, stay healthy, and avoid hospitals, doctors, and drugs. It is a conscious choice. It is up to you.

A FEW BASICS

When you have been where Jill and I have, your perspective changes, and life takes on new meaning. If you don't have health, nothing else matters, not even having a lot of wealth. It is far better to have health and wealth and the time to enjoy both. We cannot guarantee anything for anyone, but we will be happy to share the tools we carry in our backpacks. The following are just a few simple things anyone can do to begin to bring the body into balance. These may be simply a reminder for some to get back to the basics. Consider this a mini operator's manual for the body.

1. Be aware that everything that enters your being—and subsequently your body—has a positive or negative effect. This is true whether you eat it, see it, hear it, or just associate with it. This is also true even if you cannot see or hear it (i.e., the air you breathe, electronic signals, and electrical waves). Stay away from toxic people. Surround yourself with like-minded, loving beings.

2. Drink toxin-free water. Divide your weight by two. That number is the number of ounces of water you should drink each day. Almost 70 percent of the water supplied to cities has fluoride in it. The body is primarily water, and that is part of what cleanses the system of toxins. A person cannot clean out toxins with more toxins. If you take the time

to visit www.naturalnews.com/fluoride, Mike Adams will explain where fluoride comes from and just how toxic it is.

3. Good nutrition is essential to building a strong immune system. A healthy diet includes fresh organic fruits and vegetables every day. Farm-fed fish should be avoided. Nuts, seeds, grains, and root vegetables should be a large part of your diet. Stay away from processed and packaged food, most fast food, and all soda. We have seriously studied our diet, and we have proven over the years what works for us. What works for you is a study well worth undertaking.

4. The human body simply has to have the proper rest and exercise. The amount of rest is up to the individual. One will know when the body is rested. Just to maintain the immune system, exercise at least twenty minutes a day for five days a week. More is even better. A good part of that program should include aerobic exercises.

5. Learn to meditate, and schedule vacation time. The body needs to recharge.

6. You cannot afford the luxury of a negative thought.

7. Open your mind to new ideas.

8. Believe in a higher power.

9. Avoid stress as much as possible.

10. Maintain an attitude of gratitude.

When something bad happens, you can (a) let it destroy you, (b) let it define you, or (c) let it strengthen you.

Below is a list of lifestyle choices that can enhance your health and happiness.

1. Drink less alcohol and more tea.

2. Eat less meat and more veggies.

3. Eat less salt and more vinegar.

4. Eat less processed sugar and more fruit.

5. Eat less, but chew more.

6. Use less words, and take more action.
7. Be less greedy, and give more.
8. Worry less, and sleep more.
9. Drive less, and walk more.
10. Be less angry, and laugh more.

BOOKS ON NUTRITION RECOMMENDED BY GABE AND JILL

Eat to Win by Dr. Robert Haas
The Nutrition Bible by Jean Anderson and Barbara Deskins
Nature's Medicines by Harry Benjamin
Ageless Body by Chris Griscom
Nutrition against Aging by Kathleen Gross and Michael Weiner
The Target Diet by Covert Bailey
Healing with Nutrition by Jonathon V. Wright

ADDITIONAL BOOKS THAT RELATE TO THOSE RECOMMENDED PREVIOUSLY

The Edgar Casey Handbook for Health by Edgar Cayce
The Return of the Ragpicker by Og Mandino
Way of the Peaceful Warrior by Dan Millman
The Balanced Life by Alan Loy Mcginnis
The Master Speaks by Joel Goldsmith
The Colon Health Handbook by Robert Gray

More works by the previously outlined authors can be found on the Internet. Type "Natural News" into the search bar of your browser, and research what Mike Adams (the Health Ranger) has to say about health, nutrition, and many other things. Everything there is well researched and validated, and you can use the tools you find in a quest to maintain homeostasis.

As with the spiritual healers in the Philippines, when you type in Mike Adams and Natural News, a lot of negative things will come up. The negative press is placed there by the big corporations that push meds. Those corporations have an agenda that is not in the best interest of the general public. The second book will spell out our personal experience on multiple occasions where Jill and I have crossed paths with what we term the "deep state," their media, big corporations, and organizations like the AMA, AARP, the MS Society, and so many others that promote whatever it is they say they are fighting.

We will continue to pray that the light of God will one day shine on the aforementioned, as the only way they will be exposed is through illumination and education. So I say it again, love yourself just as you are, love others as you love yourself, and pray continuously for the love of God to shine through you. Jill and I have a quality of life that too few enjoy, and it stems from gratitude and love.